How to be a

How to be a Financial Goddess

Nine steps to financial security
and independence

Smita Talati

HELP YOURSELF

First published in Great Britain in 2003
This edition 2004

The right of Smita Talati to be identified as the Author
of the Work has been asserted by her in accordance
with the Copyright, Designs and Patents Act 1988.

10 9 8 7 6 5 4 3 2 1

British Library Cataloguing in Publication Data
A record for this book is available from the British Library

ISBN 0 340 86153 3

Typeset in ACaslonRegular by Avon DataSet Ltd,
Bidford-on-Avon, Warwickshire

Printed and bound in Great Britain by
Bookmarque Ltd, Croydon, Surrey

The paper and board used in this paperback are natural recyclable products
made from wood grown in sustainable forests. The manufacturing processes
conform to the environmental regulations of the country of origin.

Hodder & Stoughton
A Division of Hodder Headline Ltd
338 Euston Road
London NW1 3BH
www.madaboutbooks.com

To Dad, Mum and Ajay with love.

Contents

Acknowledgements

Thanks to my very enthusiastic editor Judith Longman for suggesting this book, and to my agent Michael Alcock for making sure I did it! Thanks to author and friend Jessica Adams for coming up with the excellent title, and to Anna Bowes and Julia Watts for proofreading.

1

Welcome to the age of the financial goddess

Like many women growing up in the 1950s, my mother never planned to have a career, buy her own flat, or travel the world after university. She graduated in India with a degree in Law in the late 1960s, married at the age of thirty and became a full-time housewife and mother in Britain.

She has always had a joint bank account, and all her savings, investments and insurances have been taken care of by my father. When he does eventually take his much-deserved retirement, she'll be entitled to a share of his final-salary pension.

How times have changed. An article in *Cosmopolitan* magazine in 1998 showed that over 95 per cent of women under the age of twenty-nine do not expect to be financially dependent on a man either now or in the future.

Girls today achieve better grades at school and obtain better degrees at university than their male counterparts. They demonstrate superior communication and networking skills in the workplace, and their ability to juggle several things at one time makes them better managers and business leaders. Although the average male professional still earns more than his female counterpart over a lifetime, the pay gap is narrowing.

All this is making women today more financially independent than ever before. More of today's first-time housebuyers are single women than men. According to recent government research, the number of single women homebuyers in Britain rose 16 per cent between 1997 and 2000, compared with a rise of just 5 per cent of single men. Even if they don't buy, women tend to fly the parental nest earlier, and miss the home comforts of having their meals cooked and washing done, less than young men.

Smart women take control of their purse strings

Television and the media may love portraying women as ditzy shopaholics, but the truth is that today's woman is very much in charge of her purse strings.

In 1998, Prudential interviewed 1019 women aged between sixteen and thirty-five about their finances, and found that more than 80 per cent of women reckoned that they were in control of their finances most, or all, of the time. Nearly half had sufficient savings to tide them over if they were to find themselves without a job for three months. A third said that if an item such as a designer suit caught their eye, they would pay for it out of their savings rather than on credit. But most illuminating of all, fewer than one in ten said they would expect the man to foot the bill at the end of the first date!

So, welcome to the age of the 'financial goddess'. Today's woman is better educated, has greater earning power, more disposable income and more spending power than her mother.

She also realises that being good with her money is not boring and dull, but sexy and smart!

Challenges for today's financial goddess

While today's woman has greater financial power than generations before her, she is also facing far greater financial challenges than they did.

Better diets, health care and standards of living mean today's crop of financial goddesses are likely to live a lot longer than their mothers or grandmothers. They therefore need to be saving a lot more for their retirement. University tuition fees and the abolition of student grants mean bright twenty-somethings can expect to be paying off five-figure student debts over several years. And soaring house prices have made it all the more difficult for first-time buyers to get a foot onto the housing ladder. Add to this a volatile stockmarket and spiralling levels of consumer debt, and it's not difficult to see why so many of us feel overwhelmed at the thought of taking control of our money.

The purpose of this book is to help you to meet these financial challenges head on, to build wealth, and achieve financial security and independence, from your early twenties to your golden years. To do this, you need to:

- devise a financial plan for life
- clear your debts
- find the money to save (today!)
- invest in the stockmarket with confidence
- build a retirement fund
- protect yourself and your loved ones.

Why you can't afford *not* to take control of your money

Why bother with all this? Because, if your finances are spiralling out of control, it will soon affect other areas of your life, like your work, health, social life and relationships.

Without a doubt, one of the most debilitating financial conditions any woman can find herself in, is uncontrolled debt. And with easy credit at our fingertips, it's an all-too-easy trap to fall into. You can be ambling along quite nicely, with your bank account more or less in the black, when suddenly an unexpected bill comes through the letterbox. You haven't got the cash to pay it 'right now', so you decide to just 'forget' about it until more money comes in.

But one missed payment soon leads to two. You think you'll catch up when your next salary cheque comes through, but by then you've slipped to square one minus two. You pay off the first bill, but you're not actually in credit till the *following* month's cheque comes through. And of course you've still got that second bill to pay. Nevertheless, you carry on spending just as you did before – the odd pair of shoes in the sales, a round of drinks after work, a birthday present for a friend. And before you know it, you're in debt again, only this time much deeper!

So you use one credit card to pay off the other, or take out yet another loan to clear the overdraft. And because you're still putting £20 a month into that savings account you've had since you were twelve, you think you're being financially responsible, by saving! A red reminder lands on your doormat and you're late for work. Or perhaps you just can't face opening it, or letting your partner see it, so you stuff it under the sofa and hope it will go away! But of course it doesn't. Time ticks by. More demands come through the letterbox. You do nothing. The creditors get angry. And then they start getting heavy, and on it goes. Research from Ohio State University shows that the stress of being in debt and financial disarray can add up to seven years onto your real age. So getting a grip on your finances will pay beauty dividends too!

Why today's financial goddess needs to save more than ever

Even if you rarely go overdrawn and always pay off those credit cards at the end of the month, are you *saving* as much as you should be? What do you fritter away money on: taxis, magazines, chocolates, cigarettes?

Tot up how much you would save in a year (in pounds and health!) if you gave up just *one* of those luxuries – £500, £700, £1,000, £1,500? What could you do with all that extra money? Have another skiing holiday, buy two new evening dresses (plus tickets to a charity ball), new bedroom furniture? Is that daily Starbucks really worth it?

Have you ever stopped to think how much you would need to maintain the same lifestyle if you stopped work now to start a family? Or how much it costs to educate two children privately and put them through university? Even more frightening, have you calculated how much you need to save to live comfortably in retirement?

What's the best way to build up a nest egg for your golden years? Given stockmarket volatility and recent financial scandals, can you trust pension providers with your money? Would you be better off putting your cash into an ISA or investing in property? Will your employer still be offering a company pension in ten years' time? Will there be a British state pension by the time you retire?

Saving for retirement is one of the greatest financial conundrums of our time, to which nobody, from the government to the financial services' industry, has yet been able to come up with a satisfactory solution. But unless we start saving *more* now, today's crop of twenty, thirty and fortysomethings could be the first generation to end up poorer than their parents.

Women make better investors than men

Now the good news. Do you realise just how well placed you, as an educated woman, are to take the lead here?

Bulls and bears (when the stockmarket soars or slumps) may once have been the preserve of pin-striped City gents, but recent research confirms what many of us have long suspected: that women make better investors than men.

In 2002, DAB Bank in Germany, which offers an online broking service through Self Trade in the UK, conducted a survey of its investors. It found that its female investors outperformed their male counterparts by a considerable margin, both in a bull market and a volatile one.

In the City of London, 10 out of 100 of the top fund managers are now women. Angela Knight, chief executive of the Association of Private Client Investment Managers, says:

Women invest with their heads while men invest with testosterone. Before a woman buys shares in a company she thoroughly researches and checks that its goods or services are worthwhile, both in the industry and in the shops – that's the best form of market testing. Women are also in the market for the long term, whereas men just tend to plump for what looks good, and listen to what their mates say in the pub!

So women are biologically programmed to play the stockmarket better than men. And yet, there's still a view out there that investing is a 'game for the boys'. Most brokers still have more male clients on their books than they do female, and men still tend to invest more money in the stockmarkets, more frequently, than women. Why is this?

Negative emotions that prevent women from becoming wealthy

In my years of writing financial makeovers for people of all ages, from all walks of life, both male and female, I've discovered three negative emotions that prevent women from becoming as wealthy as they could. These are: apathy, ignorance and fear. Let's look at each of them in turn.

Apathy: the financial ladette

The typical financially apathetic woman is the one who doesn't care if she gets into debt and can't be bothered to save or invest because she just 'knows' that 'everything will turn out alright in the end'. We could call her a financial 'ladette'.

If she finds her bank account has run dry by the end of the month, she'll just extend her overdraft. When that hits the limit, she'll just apply for a loan. Of course she wouldn't bother scouring the tables in the financial press for the cheapest deal around; the first bank to lend her the money quickly and without fuss will do.

Whenever anyone tries to tell our financial ladette that she could save herself hundreds of pounds by changing her bank account or swapping her ritzy store card for a low-interest credit card, she shrugs as if to say: What a hassle. Who has the time?

Try telling her that she ought to be saving and investing for her future, because what is she going to live on when she stops working? She'll reel off all those scare stories of financial cowboys who've run off with people's hard-earned money, and financial debacles like Equitable Life and Allied Irish Bank, faster than you can finish your sentence. Life's too short to worry about trivial things like money. She can always borrow a couple of hundred quid from her boyfriend or her mother. Why stress?

Well, one day, our financial ladette will hit thirty-five or forty, and find that while her friends have saved up deposits, bought their first home and are now on their second mortgage, she's thrown away thousands of pounds in rent and has nothing to show for it. Not even her own kettle or TV.

A group of her friends are using their savings to go on a ski chalet holiday in Verbier this winter, but her savings account is bone dry and she's got bills to pay, so she can't afford to go. By being financially apathetic, she has shortchanged herself on creating the wealth and financial freedom she deserves. Does this sound like you? Read on. The aim of this book is to inject you with a little financial get up and go!

Ignorance: an expensive mistake

But what if you *have* been saving and investing hard, but still don't seem to have anything to show for it? Your investments or pensions are worth just as much, or worse, less than you've paid into them. Chances are that you've been suffering from financial *ignorance*. While this is psychologically easier to overcome than financial apathy, undoing the damage done to your financial portfolio is a lot harder!

Financial ignorance also applies to those of us who've had our fingers burnt by falling into the hands of greedy financial advisers or bank managers who have sold us expensive, poor-performing investments and pensions. Or talked us into buying financial products like endowments or split capital investment trusts without explaining the risks.

The real sting in the tail here is that if you've bought a dud pension or insurance-based investment which is eating up such a large proportion of your monthly contributions in '*charges*' that your fund is worth less than you've put into it, the chances are there'll also be high penalties for exiting the scheme and taking your money elsewhere. In short, you could lose more money trying to move to a better product, than you would sticking with your bad egg. It's called chasing good money after bad.

The same applies to a lot of mortgages. If you're paying over the odds on a high variable rate because your fixed rate deal has come to an end, you may have to pay thousands of pounds in *redemption penalties* if you want to move your mortgage to a cheaper deal.

In such cases, you have to ask yourself, 'will the penalties outweigh the new cost savings?' Sometimes the answer is yes, it really is best to just cut your losses and run. But more often than not, the answer is 'No', because you won't actually end up saving yourself anything in return for all the stress.

By working through this book, you'll discover how to weed or prune any 'bad eggs' you may have in your financial portfolio. More importantly you'll also learn how to avoid making those mistakes again!

Fear: the greatest barrier of all

By far the greatest barrier to wealth creation for many women is financial *fear*. This can take the form of:

- fear of financial jargon
- fear of making the wrong financial decisions
- fear of taking measured financial 'risks'.

If this sounds like you, read on. The aim of this book is to help you overcome this barrier by showing you just how easy (and jargon free!) it is to take charge of your finances.

It will also explain exactly what is meant by that ultra scary term 'financial risk', so you can make an educated decision on how much risk you can afford to take. You might be surprised to discover it's a lot more than you thought!

Demystifying the jargon

Let's look at the most common financial fear of all – that of being financially illiterate.

Are you completely befuddled by what all those men and women in suits are talking about? Does your mind draw a complete blank when you hear newsreaders talking about stakeholder pensions and corporate bonds? I wouldn't be at all surprised – financial marketing guys across the international markets are paid an awful lot of money to come up with a mind-bogglingly bewildering alphabet soup of financial products. And just when you think you've got the hang of them, some government body decides to change them all again! Sometimes it seems as though financial products change more quickly than seasonal catwalk collections.

In Britain, we first had PEPs and TESSAs. Now we've got ISAs – which come as 'minis' and 'maxis' and can be 'cat-marked' or 'non cat-marked'. We can buy stakeholder pensions, SIPPs (self-invested personal pensions) or SASSes (small administered self-invested scheme). Mortgages come with fixed, variable, discounted or capped rates. We can have interest-only or capital repayment loans, tracker mortgages or Australian-style flexible mortgages. On the investment side, we can buy unit trusts, corporate bonds, with-profits bonds or fixed income funds. Then there are specially designed children's savings schemes and university fees plans bearing cosy names like Rupert the Bear, and school fees saving plans. And there are myriad insurance policies to protect everything from our homes and cars, to our own lives and those of our pets! No wonder even the professionals get confused. And if not confused, very frustrated.

Look what's inside

The first thing to understand is that in most cases these complicated sounding products don't actually mean much. Like brand packaging on supermarket shelves they are just *wrappers*.

What's important is what's *inside* them. This book will help by explaining how the financial products you need really work, and what you should look out for when you're buying one. It will also stress the importance of *shopping around* for the *best value* products.

Fear of stockmarket risk

Financial illiteracy can certainly be a stumbling block, but the one thing that really holds many women back from being as wealthy as they could be is fear of stockmarket risk.

Mention the term 'financial risk' and many women begin to shudder. They automatically assume they're going to lose all their money.

Well, they might! But with a clear head and the right technique, there's also a very good chance they'll end up a lot richer than if they'd played 'safe'.

As we said above, women who combine hard-headed investment research with feminine intuition regularly beat men at the investment game. Of course, no financial goddess should throw caution to the wind (like many male investors do!) but if she really wants to build wealth, she can't afford to avoid stockmarket risk altogether.

It's all in the *timing*

That might sound incredible given the abysmal state of the world stockmarkets at the moment. At the time of writing this, in September 2002, the FTSE has dropped to its lowest level in six years following a string of accounting scandals, corporate malpractice and financial embezzlement in the United States. There is doom and gloom all around the financial markets. Meanwhile, the housing market in some areas of Britain is growing by more than 20 per cent a year. So who in their right mind would invest in the stockmarket now?

One thing I'd like you to grasp here is that no investment, be it technology shares, American unit trusts, UK managed funds or investment property, is a fundamentally 'good' or 'bad' investment. But there is such a thing as good and bad *timing*.

If you had invested in the stockmarket at the beginning of 1997 and taken your profits in March 2000, before the technology bubble burst, you'd have doubled or tripled your money. But if you'd invested your money on a certain month in 1929, you'd have had to wait until the mid 1950s for it to have doubled! So, to be an investor of any kind, you have to be prepared to go into your chosen market (be it equities, property or wine), and come out of it, *at the right time*.

But of course, that's easier said than done, and even the professionals can't get it right all of the time. So the flip side is that you also have to invest *over* time. To create long-term wealth, you have to develop the mentality that you will take some risk, commit your money over time, but also monitor your investments so you take your profits when it is judicious to do so, rather than sit on them forever, in the hope that they'll continue going up!

How do your finances stack up?

But before you can even start contemplating exciting stuff like that, you need to know how your finances stack up at the moment.

To do this, you need to write your financial CV. This will tell you exactly what you have already in your financial portfolio, and help you decide where to go from here.

Just as a gym instructor checks your pulse and blood pressure to assess your current level of fitness before devising a suitable training programme, you need to know what state your financial portfolio is in, before you can design a financial life plan to build wealth.

Just as important as knowing what's in your portfolio, is knowing how all that stuff you've got in there actually works! Far too many people have investments, mortgages and pensions they don't really understand. The next chapter will show you, step by step, how to write your financial CV. The rest of the book will show you how to make sense of it all.

But make a start now, by just having a think about all those investments, pensions, windfall shares and insurances you've got. How well have they performed? Are you pleased you bought them? (Why did you buy them? Was it through apathy, ignorance, fear?) It would be even more helpful to think about where all those financial statements and bits of paper are. Can you get your hands on them? This will help you to write your CV much quicker, and give you a head start in financial housekeeping!

The five financial vitamins

There are five financial 'vitamins' we all need to build wealth and achieve financial security. These are:

- savings
- investments
- mortgages
- pensions
- insurances.

The following chapters will look at each of these vitamins in detail, but let's get a broad overview of them and how they function in our financial diet:

1) Savings: *cash is queen*

The foundation for wealth creation and financial security is *saving*. Saving is not the same as investing. Savings will not make you wealthy over the long term. What they will do is provide you with a financial cushion on which to fall back if you lose your job, need to get your car fixed, or just want to go on holiday.

When we talk about 'saving' we mean putting away a proportion of our disposable money into a high-interest deposit account or a cash ISA. Savings are safe because the money remains in cash and we know we can always get our hands on it quickly. Short of the entire banking system collapsing it's pretty much impossible to lose your cash savings!

So savings are often referred to as 'rainy day funds' or 'cash reserves'. They give us financial and psychological security. If you know you have the money put by to fix your boiler before it's even broken, it gives you an immense sense of freedom and confidence.

Our grandmothers were great savers, but tempting offers for easy credit and a 'buy now, save later' mentality means that as a nation we're losing that good old-fashioned habit of saving for the short term. A decade ago, the average British adult squirrelled away nearly 10 per cent of their annual income; today we put aside just 5.2 per cent. Women on the continent save more than British women. The chapter on savings will show you how to find the money to start saving today, and how interest accumulates.

2) Investments: *get rich slow*

Saving is also the first rung of the investment pyramid. While savings provide you with a financial cushion, investments are the financial vehicles that will make you rich over the long term.

According to the Barclay Equity-Gilt study, one of the most influential reports on stockmarket returns, the average return on equity investments over the past ten years has been 8.6 per cent compared with just 4.8 per cent return on cash.

The chapter on investing will show you how to create an investment plan for life and how to turn your first £1000 investment into a six-figure lump sum over the years. Investing means putting money into the stockmarket, and this involves taking financial risk.

But forget any notions of 'doubling your money' overnight. The investment philosophy of the financial goddess is to *get rich slow*. This means building up an investment pyramid layer by layer and increasing the amount of financial risk you take as the value of your investment portfolio grows.

As I'm sure you've heard many times before, the value of stockmarket investments can go down as well as up. However, as we said earlier, one of the greatest protections against stock-market volatility is *time*. So the younger you are, and the *longer* you have to save, the more money you can afford to tie up in higher-risk equity investments.

All about ISAs

For British investors, the best way to invest in the stockmarket is to put your money in an ISA (individual savings account) so the money grows tax-free.

You can put up to £3000 into a *mini* cash ISA and £3000 into a *mini* stockmarket-based ISA each year. Or you can put £7000 into a *maxi* ISA.

There's a huge variety of ISA investments on offer out there. You can invest in numerous different territories, like the UK, Europe, America and Asia, and different market sectors, like banks and insurance companies, technology, media and food.

We'll explain a lot more about ISAs in the chapters on saving and investing.

3) Mortgages: *a goddess' home is her palace*

The third financial vitamin is mortgages. Unless you or your partner are expecting a six-figure bonus or inheritance, you'll need to take out a *mortgage* to buy your home.

Property has proven to be an excellent investment in Britain, particularly in London and the South-east where, in many areas, house prices have doubled within five years.

But runaway prices have also made it much more difficult for first-time buyers to get onto that all-important first rung of the ladder. In June 2002 the average price of a property in Greater London was £198,000 – more than nine times the national average salary! And the average age of a first-time housebuyer in Britain is now thirty-four.

In days gone by, lenders would advance a couple 2.5 times their joint annual income and a single person 3.25 times their annual income. But high house prices mean that many first-time buyers need to borrow an awful lot more than that to get onto the property ladder.

Interest rates are currently at their lowest for forty years, so mortgages are more affordable than ever before. Some lenders will now offer first-time buyers mortgages of up to six times their annual salary. Others will extend the loan period from the typical twenty-five-year term to thirty, thirty-five and even forty years.

If you're a first-time buyer with itchy feet, it's tempting to jump at these offers if buying a property on the traditional model is beyond your reach. But think long and hard before you commit yourself to taking on so much debt. Just like stockmarket investments, property prices can crash too.

The last serious property crash was of course in the late eighties. In 1988, house prices across Britain rose a staggering

34 per cent, making the average London home worth £105,000. But interest rate hikes and economic recession brought the market crashing down again, and by 1993, average London house prices had fallen to £75,000, and did not recover to their 1989 levels until early 1998, by which time 450,000 homes had been repossessed.

4) Pensions: aging abundantly

Hardly a day goes by when the subject of pensions does not hit the news, and rightly so. With life expectancy increasing, many of us can expect to spend twenty or thirty years in retirement. But with company pension schemes being axed at the rate of knots, personal pensions underfunded, and no guarantee of a state pension in future years, Britain is sitting on a pensions timebomb.

Building up a retirement fund is an expensive business, so the sooner you start the better. As a rough guide, the Financial Services Authority calculates that if you start saving £50 a month at the age of twenty-five, you'll have a pension income of £310 a month at the age of sixty-five. Put it off till thirty-five, and you'll get just £191 a month. Leave it till you're forty-five, and you'll have just £105 a month.

Not only are pensions expensive, they can also be complicated. For many people, the biggest incentive of saving into a pension is that it offers tax relief. For every £77 a basic rate tax payer saves, the government makes it up to £100.

But there are many downsides: you cannot access money saved into a pension fund until the age of fifty. You can then take 25 per cent of the fund as a tax-free cash lump sum, but are obliged to buy an 'annuity', which will give you an annual income for the rest of your life, with the remaining 75 per cent.

But perhaps the greatest drawback to buying an annuity is that if you die prematurely, the life assurance company from which you purchased your annuity simply pockets the money you've been saving all those years.

So, many people are ditching pensions and turning to other vehicles like ISAs and property to build up a retirement nest egg. The chapter on pensions will explain the various ways of building a retirement fund, from occupational company schemes to personal stakeholder pensions, and the impact of taking a career break to start a family.

5) Insurance: *take care of yourself*

The final financial 'vitamin' is *insurance*. Financial salesmen love selling insurance policies because they bring in lots of commission. No financial goddess should neglect her responsibilities by under-insuring herself. But neither should she waste money on policies she doesn't need.

If you are single and do not have dependants, you do not need life insurance. If you have children under the age of eighteen you most certainly do. Homeowners need building and contents insurance, but will generally get a better deal if they shop online rather than buy whatever is offered by their bank or mortgage lender. Drivers need motor insurance.

Many women ask me about health and dental insurance. Some employers offer this as a company perk. But it can be expensive to buy yourself, and you need to check the small print to ensure that it does not exclude medical conditions you may wish to claim for.

The younger you are when you take out a health insurance policy, the cheaper your monthly premiums will be. But it still won't come cheap, and you may well decide to just save into an investment scheme, so the money is there if you need it, but you can spend it on something else if you don't!

The financial goddess –
from graduate to grandma

So now you've got a brief insight into the financial vitamins a financial goddess needs, and the role they have in building wealth and financial security. But simply stuffing your portfolio with loads of the right vitamins and then forgetting about them, isn't any good. They'll quickly go stale! Managing your finances isn't something you pick up one weekend a year and then put away in a drawer: like exercise and diet, it's an ongoing task that needs to be kept under constant *review*.

Your financial circumstances will change throughout your life: leaving university and starting work, getting married or moving in with a partner, starting a family, returning to work, meeting the needs of a growing family, funding your children through university and eventually enjoying a wealthy retirement! Single women will of course have a lot more money to spend on themselves than those with children, but they'll need to meet the full cost of mortgages, bills and pensions themselves.

If a live-in relationship, or worse, a marriage, breaks down, it will wreak havoc with your finances, as well as your emotions. If you've always left all the financial arrangements to your husband or boyfriend, you might find the thought of having to take control of the purse strings and fend for yourself and children, scary. This book will help you pick up the pieces, and put you on the road to financial independence.

Why you deserve to be a financial goddess

Good financial management is essential for today's woman. It's also easy and fun. Many women who previously thought that money management was 'boring' and 'difficult', find themselves completely hooked once they get started. They go on to form investment clubs, and take an active role in looking after their family's finances.

But the cost of ignoring your finances is huge. If you don't bother saving and investing in your twenties and thirties, you'll shortchange yourself on enjoying the wealth you deserve in your later years.

If you allow your finances to get out of control by committing yourself into a huge mortgage, or not adjusting your spending according to new circumstances, you'll quickly find yourself being pulled into a downward spiral of debt. This will not only harm your finances, but also your career, health and relationships.

Every woman deserves to have the confidence that comes from knowing she has savings of her own put by, can invest and insure herself, and is on track to building up a healthy retirement fund. And every woman has the ability to do it. There's no 'mystique' to learning to become wealthy, and it's nothing to do with luck either. It just takes time, practice, a little knowledge and lots of discipline. So let's get started!

2

The five ages of the financial goddess

This chapter is all about financial planning. Women are naturally good planners – it's what helps us juggle careers, families, relationships, hobbies and a social life. As we said in the last chapter, financial goddesses don't just pick up their finances every once in a while like a piece of knitting, they manage them on a regular basis. In short, they follow a holistic financial *lifeplan*.

Why do you need a financial plan?

Why do you need to plan? Isn't it enough to make sure you pay the mortgage on time, go easy on the old credit card, and perhaps take out a choice investment or two when you get an unexpected windfall?

No. That's called taking an ad hoc approach to financial management. It may achieve short-term financial goals, but just as a trip to the gym once every six months won't keep your body in tip-top condition, the 'if and when' attitude to financial management won't give you long-term financial security and freedom.

To live the life of a financial goddess, you need an ongoing financial lifeplan that will look after you from your early twenties till you're grey and old. This means having a set of financial goals for the short, medium and long term.

Without a coherent financial plan in place, you risk going through life simply making ends meet (if you're lucky) and falling into long-term debt and poverty (if you're not!). You might make the right ad hoc decisions every now and then: open a high-interest savings account, double your money with a few choice shares, save a few thousand pounds by switching mortgages. But without a plan you'll go through life swimming aimlessly through the financial jungle, rather than reaching for stars. Financial goddesses don't pick up the financial crumbs, they build wealth!

The need for flexibility

Of course, life doesn't always work out the way we want it to, and even the best-laid plans can go wrong, so your financial plan – and the financial products you choose to put in it – needs to be flexible.

Your financial plan should be able to see you through all the financial roundabouts, one-way streets and spaghetti junctions of, say, a house sale falling through, the unexpected costs of starting a family, falling ill and becoming unable to work, or losing jobs (or a partner). Lack of flexibility is one of the main reasons I hate endowment policies.

Adapting your finances to new circumstances

The typical twenty-first-century financial goddess will go through several financial life 'ages', each posing new financial challenges. What separates a good financial goddess from a mediocre one is that the latter adapts her spending patterns and financial strategies to her new life circumstances, while the former just carries on the way she always has done regardless! This is easier said than done, and is as much a psychological as a financial feat.

It has been proven, time and time again, that you're most likely to fall into debt and financial disarray after downshifting to a lower paid job, falling ill, starting a family, or getting divorced, when you may be tempted to carry on with your old spending habits even though your financial circumstances have changed.

Some women naturally possess the knack of spending according to their means – they're off to a head start. Others need to learn and practise it over and over again, until it becomes second nature.

The cost of *not* adapting to your new financial circumstances

Let me give you an example. Say you're a high-flying advert-ising executive, used to eating out several times a week, having endless romantic weekends away and buying every type of new shoe as soon as it comes into fashion. You give up work for eighteen months to have your first child. You've got the maternity wear, but the change in your financial circumstances hasn't quite sunk in yet. Each time you wander down the High Street, you believe you're still the old high-earning executive, and carry on spending like a *Sex in the City* goddess – a new dress in the sales, an armful of glossy magazines each time you pass through a railway station, gossipy lunches with a friend in the pricey cafe down the road, a stack of books on the three-for-two offers. The thing is, it all seems to cost a lot more than it did when you were a happy-go-lucky, childless couple.

That's because the spare cash you used to fritter away on yourself and your partner when you had two good incomes and just two mouths to feed, is now needed to pay for the larger mortgage, baby clothes and car seats. Carry on spending the way you did before, and you'll find yourself constantly operating on an overdraft and needing to take out a loan just to meet your family's day-to-day expenses.

You may be tempted to skimp on essentials like life insurance. But if you lost your partner in an accident and weren't covered, you could end up paying the price for the rest of your life. By not adapting your spending habits and financial priorities, you risk putting not only your own financial future, but also those of your child and partner in danger. That's mad and bad.

Similarly, if you quit your job to travel, or take on a mortgage which is way beyond your means, you'll quickly find yourself spiralling into debt as the cost of surveys, insurances, stamp duty and furniture add up. Time plays funny tricks with your finances. Like a game of snakes and ladders, it takes no time at all to slide down into the red, but it's a hell of a job climbing back up onto the straight and narrow again!

Five ages of the financial goddess

So how can you ensure you adapt your finances according to your new life situations? Well, forewarned is forearmed, so below we give portraits of the typical *'financial ages'* today's woman is likely to go through and the key financial 'must haves' we think you should acquire during that age.

Cappuccino goddess

These are not easy times for twentysomething women. University fees, abolition of maintenance grants, and a slack job market mean recent graduates are likely to be paying off colossal debts during their first few working years.

Balancing the books

Students graduating in London in 2001 had average debts of £13,000; the figure was slightly less outside the capital, though with house prices in many areas creeping frighteningly close to London levels, new graduates nationwide are feeling the pinch.

Against this, the national average graduate starting salary in 2002 was just £13,422 (rising to between £20,000 and £25,000 for high-fliers in London). So making the books balance as a newly qualified 23-year-old can seem like a near impossible task.

Piling on the debt

We also live in an aggressively consumerist society, in which easy credit is always up for grabs. The Consumer Credit Counselling Service reports that debt among modern live-for-today under-thirties is skyrocketing, with many young women up to £30,000 in the red, and on 'debt management plans' which will last until their late thirties.

This is not a good way to start your financial lifeplan if you want to buy a house, get married and start a family. Some debt is unavoidable for students these days, but if your spending has spiralled out of control, read the next chapter which gives a five-point plan to clearing debt and staying out of the red for good. And no matter how good an investor you think you are, don't be tempted to beat the rate you're paying on your debts by investing, or even saving. It won't work and you'll be in even more of a muddle than you were before you started. The next chapter will show you how to find the best credit cards and how to bargain like a shopping goddess!

You're more likely to get divorced than change your bank account!

One of the greatest champions of financial apathy is the fact that a woman is more likely to get divorced than change her bank account! It's easy to have the same inertia about ditching usurious credit cards, mortgages and dud investments – so much paperwork, time and hassle. So one of the most important things to do in your twenties is to make sure you have the right bank accounts, savings products and credit cards for your needs – and needless to say they might not be the same ones Mum and Dad have got!

The next chapter will explain exactly how current accounts work, how cheques are cleared, the difference between standing orders and direct debits, car finance and travel shopping, so you are the mistress of your day-to-day finances from day one. Many of the best financial deals these days are to be found online, so you will also learn to become a financial e-chick!

Getting on the housing ladder

With rocketing house prices, the average age of the first-time buyer in Britain is thirty-four. As reported in chapter 1, there has been a substantial increase in the number of women buyers – a quarter of London's first-time buyers are now women. Another emerging trend is students becoming property landlords.

But with homes in Britain now less affordable for first-time buyers than they have been for a generation, getting onto the first rung of the housing ladder can seem like an elusive dream. Many women are therefore deciding to club together and buy with friends, or take advantage of government initiatives like shared ownership. The chapter on mortgages will explain the pros and cons of doing this.

Many mortgage lenders will now advance young people 100 per cent mortgages. Some have been reported to be lending new graduates six or seven times their salary. If you're confident you'll be able to pay the repayments whatever happens, fine. But if you're at all doubtful (and most of us are) don't do it. I've heard of girls who won't be able to buy a new pair of shoes for the next five years because they've been so desperate to get onto the property ladder, they've mortgaged themselves to the hilt.

There *are* still property bargains to be had if you're prepared to look. If buying in the area you've had your heart set on means stretching yourself too far, look elsewhere, or at other types of property, or wait until you're on a better financial footing.

Pensions

Pension planning was once a must-do for twenty somethings. In theory it still is! If you can afford to top up your employer's scheme or start saving into your own then *do*!

With a dwindling work force, life expectancy increasing (the average American can expect to live to the ripe old age of seventy-seven), and employers closing occupational pension schemes, building up a sufficient retirement fund is going to be a big financial headache for all of us.

But, in reality, student debt and rising property prices mean most twentysomethings these days have to concentrate on clearing debts and getting onto the first rung of the housing ladder, and so they delay pension planning till their thirties.

Financial must dos for the cappuccino goddess:

- Find the right bank account, savings products and credit cards.
- Clear your student debts.
- Build up a deposit for your first home.
- Become a financial e-chick.
- Acquire credit card power and become a shopping goddess!

Sex in the City goddess

If you're a single high-earning woman in your thirties or forties, you're probably having the time of your life financially. Having escaped paying university tuition fees, you should be blissfully free of student debt (if you're not, you've got some explaining to do!). You're likely to be at the height of your earning power, and free of family responsibilities. You probably have more disposable income now than you will have at any other stage in your life.

You can afford better holidays, furniture, the gym membership, beauty treatments and clothes than you could in your twenties. You may have bought your own flat and have a portfolio of savings and investments. Congratulations!

Build a cash reserve equal to three months' earnings

But don't get carried away with partying. Now that you're on a better financial footing, it's time to undertake some serious long-term financial planning.

First off, build up a *cash reserve* equivalent to at least three months' salary. This is 'rainy day' money you can draw on if your car breaks down, you lose your job, or just fancy another holiday. As we said in chapter 1: *cash is queen!*

Get cracking with the pension planning

The next most important thing is *pension planning*. Until the age of thirty-five, you can put up to 17.5 per cent of your earnings into a pension and receive tax relief on it. Whether you choose to save into a traditional pension plan or build up the money through ISAs or property, you should aim to salt away at least 15 per cent of your income.

Research from the Financial Services Authority (FSA), Britain's financial regulator, found that nearly half of young people in Britain under the age of thirty-four did not have a pension. More worryingly, it said that among those who did, many had started saving too late, or did not bother checking how well their funds have been performing.

The watchdog believes that many of us are storing up for ourselves a 'nasty shock' because we unwittingly believe that we'll have paid off all our debts and have saved enough to enjoy a better standard of living in retirement than in work!

Don't get caught out. Pensions aren't magic. Building up a retirement fund is a long, expensive business which requires careful planning and management. The pensions chapter will explain ways of building retirement options, with some serious number crunching to show just how much you need to be saving to build that elusive nest egg.

Protect your finances if you're co-habiting or dating

If you're co-habiting or dating, you need to protect your finances accordingly. Under English law, co-habitees with joint property and investments do not have the same rights as married couples, even if they have children. If you are sharing a home or bank account but aren't married, read the section in the last chapter on money, relationships and avoiding STDs (sexually transmitted debt!).

Taking a financial sabbatical

A recent article in the *Daily Mail* described today's thirtysomethings as the *Cold Feet* generation, unwilling to put up with long working hours in uninspiring jobs or stay in dead-end relationships. Our mothers would never have dared to chuck in their jobs (or marriages) to go travelling or become self-employed, just because they were bored! But we're very much a 'want it all' generation.

While writing this, I can think of at least three friends who've become temporary 'financial Cinderellas' because they've left well-paid jobs to go off travelling, set up their own businesses or go back to university.

If you want to take a financial 'sabbatical', plan it so that you've saved a little first, and remember to adapt your spending habits according to your new financial situation. (If you're planning to quit your job as a lawyer to write your first novel, pizza and a cheap bottle of plonk will be more your new style than sushi and cocktails – at least until it becomes a bestseller!) As we said, learning to adapt to new financial situations is what marks out a great financial goddess from an average one.

Start investing in the stockmarket for the long term

As well as pension planning, you should start saving regularly into a *stockmarket-linked* fund. As we illustrated in the first chapter, historically, stockmarket returns have nearly always outperformed cash over the medium to long term (for example, over five years). Of course there's no guarantee, and stockmarkets in America, Britain and continental Europe have been depressed for many months with little immediate relief in sight. But financial history does have a habit of repeating itself, and the longer the term of your investment the better. As we said, fear of stockmarket risk is one of the key things that holds women back from being as wealthy as they could be.

The best way to invest in the stockmarket in Britain is through a tax-free ISA. The chapter on investing will show you how to play the stockmarket like a goddess. Finally, your early thirties are also a good time to consider buying health insurance if you want it, as premiums will be quite low.

Must dos for Sex in the City goddesses in their thirties and forties:

- Build up a cash reserve equivalent to three months' salary.
- Save at least 15 per cent of your income for your retirement.
- Start regular savings in a stockmarket ISA.
- If you are co-habiting, protect yourself from STDs.
- Build up a cash 'kitty' if you're planning a 'financial sabbatical'.
- Consider buying health insurance.

Gap shopper goddess

Starting a family is one of the biggest financial shocks you're likely to face as a financial goddess. Relationship counsellors say more couples argue about money than they do about sex and housework!

Joint or separate accounts?

The first decision to make is whether to have joint or separate bank accounts. Most couples these days like to have a little bit of financial independence, even if they're not working. A strategy that usually works well, is to retain separate current accounts for your salaries and personal spending, and each contribute to a joint deposit account to pay for bills, furniture and holidays.

Living off one salary

If you're planning to give up work to start a family and are worried about how you'll cope, do a dummy run for six months: live off one salary and save the other in a tax-free ISA or high-interest savings account. Not only will it help budget when the baby comes along, you'll also have built up a nice little nest egg!

Savings for your children

You'll probably want to open a savings account or investment for your newborn. This is an excellent way to build up a lump sum for their university education, wedding or first home, as the money can grow over many years.

As a general rule, opening an investment or savings account for your baby is no different to opening one for yourself, so avoid anything that gives a free teddy bear or has a cosy sounding name like the 'Paddington Bear protected stock-market fund'. As children are non-tax payers, they can earn up to £100 interest tax free. Grandparents can also gift up to £3000 a year to their grandchildren tax free – and it's a good idea for them to invest this in a fairly 'risky' stockmarket investment.

A recent report also showed that today's grandparents save their families a whopping £1bn in babysitting costs a year. The cost of hiring a nanny is exorbitant, so yet another reason not to fall out with your mother-in-law!

The effect on your pension

Taking a career break is a difficult decision for women professionally and financially. It is during these years that you are most likely to fall behind your male counterparts in the salary stakes and lose several years' pension planning. If you can afford it, continue to make contributions to your pension, as it is a very tax-efficient way of investing. Non-earning spouses and children are also entitled to have a stakeholder pension, which guarantees low charges.

Insure yourself and your family

As we said earlier, life insurance is essential for every family. Many employers offer life insurance of up to 3.5 times salary. If yours doesn't, you'll need to take out your own. Life insurance will give your partner a lump sum to take care of himself and your children in the event of your untimely death.

The cheapest form of life insurance is *decreasing term insurance*. If you are a full-time mother, you may also want to take out *family income benefit* which will pay out an annual income for a full-time housekeeper or nanny if anything happens to you.

British insurance firm Legal & General, which conducts an annual survey 'Value of a Mum', has calculated that the cost of a mother's work in bringing up a child to the age of eighteen, is about £22,355 a year.

School fees

If you want to educate your children privately, start saving into a stockmarket-linked ISA *now*. The cost of educating one child from the age of five to eighteen can be as much as £100,000. Even if you don't opt to go private, the cost of uniforms, books and schools trips at a local state school can add up to £15,000 over eleven years.

Unless you've got very generous parents or are expecting a huge inheritance, it's unrealistic to expect to have saved up eleven years' worth of school fees by your child's fifth birthday, so don't go overboard. Professional couples often find that as their careers progress and incomes rise, they can afford to pay a good chunk of the school fees out of their salaries, though it's always painful!

As with children's savings, avoid any investment schemes packaged as 'school fees savings plan'. Monthly savings into good stockmarket ISAs producing an average return of 9 per cent a year, tax free, are hard to beat.

Estate planning

Rising property prices mean many young families have been pushed into the 'inheritance tax' bracket, and worry about how to protect their estate from death duties. If you die, any part of your estate worth over £250,000, will be subject to an inheritance tax of 40 per cent. In reality, there are many ways you can bypass this, which is why it is often said that 'inheritance tax' is really a voluntary tax.

But it can be complicated, so this is one area where you should seek good advice. Basically, you have two options: organise insurances which will help your children '*meet*' the tax bill, or gift parts of your estate to your children so you '*beat*' the bill. But many people seem cautious about adopting the latter strategy. Not for nothing do pundits say inheritance tax planning is only a problem for those who distrust their heirs more than they dislike the Inland Revenue!

Must dos for gap shopper goddesses:

- Set up a joint account for bills, household expenses and holidays.
- Do a dummy run for six months if you're planning to stop work.
- Buy adequate life insurance.
- Maintain pension contributions or long-term savings.
- Start a children's saving plan.

- If you want to buy private education, start saving now!
- Start estate planning.

Loft converter goddess

Meeting the needs of a growing family, ensuring you are saving enough for your retirement and insuring yourself adequately in your forties and fifties is a real financial challenge.

You'll have financial demands firing on all cylinders. Your teenagers will have independent ideas on how much pocket money they need for clothes, music and mobile phones. Meanwhile, you're already slaving away all the hours God sends to pay their school and university fees, while paying a larger mortgage and possibly also funding a loft conversion!

The car breaks down and the boiler needs replacing. You and your husband could do with another holiday, but not in peak season. You're certainly looking forward to taking it easy in your golden years, but will you ever have saved enough?

Stockmarkets are plunging, life insurance companies are cutting bonuses at the rate of knots, and your pension provider's kindly gone bust. You'd be forgiven for thinking you may as well have taken your money down to the bookie's. You've seen your mother-in-law suffer at the hands of Britain's creaking NHS and never want that to happen to you.

Private health insurance is a must, you say to yourself, but then you find the policy won't cover you for cancer, and the ones that do are ridiculously expensive. Just to top it all, you might also be rebuilding a new life after divorce, or your partner's redundancy. What's a woman to do?

Monitor your investments

Well, if you've been following the advice so far, you should have built up a reasonable nest egg of investments over the past ten or fifteen years, and now might be a good time to take some of the profits – or at least move them into cash so you can get your hands on it.

Investing is not some pointless academic exercise. It's about directing your money into vehicles that will make it work harder for you, so you can afford to do things you wouldn't have been able to if you'd spent it as soon as it came in. As we said, you have to be prepared to monitor your investments, and take profits when they are there, and when you need them, and that might be now.

Pack money into your pension

Pension planning is vital for women in their forties. If you've neglected it in your thirties, start today. If your employer still offers an occupational scheme, you'd be mad not to join it (unless you know you're going to leave within two years in which case you wouldn't be able to transfer your pension benefits). Not only will your employer contribute to the pension scheme, it will include some life insurance, a pension if you have to retire early due to ill health, and pension for your partner and dependants when you die. However, a raft of British blue-chip companies have closed down their schemes to new entrants in the past couple of years, so many employees have lost one of the best company perks around.

Write a tax-efficient will

You should also write a tax-efficient will, known as a discretionary will trust (also known as a Loan Plan will) or your children and other beneficiaries will have to pay tax at 40 per cent on all your assets worth more than £250,000. By writing a tax-efficient trust will, when you or your partner dies, £250,000 of your assets are left to the trust and transferred to the surviving spouse, who promises to repay the trust the £250,000 on death. But when he or she dies, his estate is reduced by £250,000 – so the surviving spouse will have had use of your assets without restrictions, and your children will inherit your estate tax free when the second parent dies.

If a couple with a house and assets worth £500,000 both wrote Loan Plan wills, they would have passed on no inheritance tax liability to their children when the second spouse dies, saving them a £100,000 tax bill.

Must dos for loft convertor goddesses:
- Take profits from investments as you need them.
- Save at least 15 per cent of your income into a retirement fund.
- Ensure you have sufficient life insurance.
- Write a tax-efficient will.
- Start saving for children's university fees.
- Consider buying family health insurance.

Empty-nest goddess

Most people hope that by their mid-fifties they will have paid off their mortgage and their children will be earning their own living. 'Baby boomers', as today's generation of fiftysomethings are known, are apparently having the time of their life, enjoying cruises, posh cars and second homes.

But the future is not so bright for those of us who have several years to go to retirement. As we said earlier, unless we start saving like mad (or working till we're seventy), we're likely to encounter a huge pension deficit. As we are likely to live longer than our parents, we'll also need more money for health care in our old age.

Your money makeover

So now you've got your financial lifeplan sorted out, it's time to put the right savings and investments into it.

As we said in the first chapter, to keep your finances under review, you need to compile your financial CV, and update it at regular intervals. This will give you a clear snapshot of how your finances stack up and the areas you need to work on. Writing your CV, warts and all, will make you face up to your finances, and see them in a fresh light.

Look in the financial mirror

As you're writing your own financial CV, ask yourself questions. If you're in your mid-thirties and don't have a single savings account or investment to your name, why? Is it out of apathy, ignorance or fear?

If you are in your forties and still a pension virgin, is it because you took several years off work to start a family and never had the spare cash to put into a retirement fund? If you've got a dud investment, or an endowment that won't pay off your mortgage, is it because you were unwittingly sold it out of ignorance?

As with so many other things in life, it's really only when you write down your finances that you see them (and your financial self) for what they really are. It's only then that you realise that despite the fact that you've been paying £150 a month into a pension for the past thirteen years, it's not worth much more than it would be if you'd put it in the building society. Or it suddenly dawns on you that your variable rate mortgage is costing you thousands of pounds more than a cheap penalty-free fixed rate. So much more in fact that you could have paid for a second holiday with the difference! Or that you're trying to save £50 a month in an investment while paying interest on an overdraft! Where's the sense in that?

Any solutions?
Even before reading any further, can you think of any ways to improve your CV? Perhaps you could earn an extra £100 a year in interest just by putting the spare cash in your current account into an ISA. Easy!

Are you paying £100 a month into a regular savings investment scheme, while sitting on a £2000 overdraft for which you are paying a whopping 15 per cent a month interest? Trying to save and invest before paying off your debts is like trying to run before you can walk. Or working out in the gym while munching on a greasy whopper Mac and double fries – totally crazy and counterproductive.

You can't jump from square minus three to square eight, so don't even try. Pay off your debts, *before* trying to save, or you'll get yourself into a real muddle.

The art of good financial housekeeping

Whether you hate or love housework, to become a financial goddess you need to master the art of good financial housekeeping.

Finding stuff!
Of course, the main reason why good housekeeping is important is so that you can get your hands on information and statements when you need them. There's no point opening a cash ISA if you lose your passbook and can't get any money out! You'll need to track down all sorts of bits of paper to write your full financial CV, and if you've been neglecting your finances, this might turn into a bit of a treasure hunt! It might also throw up a few surprises. You might remember childhood savings accounts or investments your relatives bought you several years ago, but you've since forgotten. There are several billion pounds lying in dormant accounts, investment, inheritance and pension plans, which go unclaimed every year. So if you think you might have an old savings account or pension somewhere, read the box on 'Unclaimed Fortunes' in the next chapter to find out how to go about retrieving them. You might get a nice surprise!

Divide and file

To ensure that you don't lose any vital passbooks or statements again, get them organised. *Divide* all your bills, savings accounts, current account and credit card statements, pensions, insurances and investments into sections and *file* them away. This will also help you if you hate financial jargon and don't think you understand any of it.

Even better, colour code your finances!

In 1997, I interviewed a lovely lady who ran her own theatre company. She told me that as an art student she had suffered from 'numerical dyslexia'. She used to work on a market stall and was constantly giving people the wrong change! But after getting married, she decided to apply her artistic talents to her finances, by colour coding. So she set up a red folder for her pension, a blue one for her mortgage, a green one for her savings, and so on. As actors, neither she nor her husband earned a fortune, but they'd always paid their mortgage and had an annual holiday, and her coloured-coded system means she now finds managing her finances a doddle!

Get your finances online

Busy women these days don't have the time to be messing around with lots of bits of paper, so an even better way to keep your financial documents in order is to save them all on a computer. As we said earlier, some of the best financial deals are online, so the next chapter will show you how to become a financial e-chick. Also, make sure you delete financial junk mail (online and off!).

Your financial CV

Now it's time to write that CV. So take a sheet of A4 paper, or even better, set up a new computer document. Writing your CV may take a little time, and you might not want to do it in one go, but you can't progress any further till you've done it, so don't be tempted to skip it!

Personal information

Name:
Age:
Occupation:
Income (single and joint):

Mortgage/Rent

a) Monthly repayments: how much are you *paying* each month in mortgage or rent?

b) How much did you *borrow* when you took out the mortgage? How many *years* do you have left before you pay it off? (Most mortgages are repaid over twenty-five years, but younger homeowners may have taken a thirty-year loan to reduce their monthly repayments. Older borrowers may have a fifteen- or even ten-year loan so they are debt free by the time they retire.)

c) Is it a *repayment* or *interest–only* mortgage?

d) What type of *rate* are you paying? E.g. a *'fixed rate'* for one, three, or five years, or a *'discounted rate'* (usually a couple of percentage points below the variable rate); *capped rate*, a variable rate mortgage which cannot go above a certain 'cap', or are you paying the lender's *standard variable rate*?

e) Are there any *redemption penalties*? If you have a fixed rate mortgage, you're likely to be locked into paying the lender's variable rate for two or even five years. If you pull out of this, you'll be penalised by having to pay several months' interest. There's no point switching to a cheaper mortgage, if it will cost you the same amount upfront to move. Read the small print on your mortgage contract, or phone your lender, and make a note of what redemption penalties you would have to pay if you moved your mortgage.

f) If you have an *endowment mortgage*, make a note of the name of the insurance provider. Also note i) your monthly premiums, ii) how long the policy has been running for, iii) how much you borrowed when you bought your home, iv) if the endowment is on track to pay off this amount, and v) if not, what is the estimated shortfall?

Savings

a) Make a note of all the savings accounts you have with banks or building societies. Note *how much* you have in each account and what *rate of interest* you are earning on them.
b) Do the same for any cash ISAs.
c) List any National Savings bonds – how long do you have till maturity and what rate of interest are you earning?
d) How much *surplus cash* have you got sitting in your current account, and how much *interest* is it earning?

Investments

a) List all *stockmarket-based* investments here: unit trusts, investment trusts, PEPs, ISAs, shares.
b) Make a note of the names of the *funds*. How much is each one currently worth? (Most investment houses send half-yearly statements, so you'll find the information there.)
c) *How much* have you saved into this fund so far? (If it's a regular savings plan, have you been putting £50 or £100 into it for several years?) If you invested a lump sum, *when* did you make the investment?
d) Make a list of all the *charges* that are deducted from your investments. Things to look for are: an *initial* charge, and an *annual management* charge. How much are they?

e) *Where* is your fund invested? Is it a UK blue-chip fund, international fund, technology fund?

f) If you own shares: list each company and *how many* you have in them. What price did you *buy* them at, and what is their price today?

Pensions

a) Are you a member of a company pension scheme? If so, what sort of scheme is it: stakeholder, money purchase, final-salary (turn to the chapter on pensions if you need an explanation of these)?

b) How much does your employer contribute to the fund and how much do you contribute?

c) How many years' contributions do you have?

d) If you are married, what sort of pension does your husband have? If you are divorced, what entitlement do you have to any pension your ex-husband built up?

e) If you have *personal pensions*: note the name of the provider and the *funds* you have been investing in.

f) How much do you *contribute* a month, and *how long* have you been contributing for?

g) What are the *charges* on your personal pension? Are there any *exit penalties*?

Insurances

a) Life insurance: *how much* are you insured for? Is it enough?

b) What are your *monthly premiums*?

c) Do the same for your *home* and *car insurance*.

d) If you have health insurance, note the *premiums*. What is the excess you would have to pay before the insurer would pay up, and are there any *exclusions*?

Debts

a) If you are overdrawn, by *how much*, and what *interest rate* are you paying?

b) If you have loans, list them here, and write down your *outstanding debts* on each, and again the *interest rate* you are paying.

c) Also make a note of any *penalties* you will face if you want to pay off the loan early.

Credit cards

a) List all credit cards and store cards on which you *do not* pay off the balance in full each month.

b) Note down the *APR* (Annual Percentage Rate) you are paying.

c) Now tot up *how much interest* you've paid on each card over the past year (ouch!).

Your financial goals

Now write down your financial goals. We could all do with more money now but remember your financial lifeplan and think long term.

Split your financial goals up into:

a) short (in the next five years)
b) medium (five to ten years)
c) long-term (over ten years).

Give as much information as possible about your goals. If you want to buy your first home within the next eighteen months, make a note of where and what sort of property: two-bedroom garden flat, newly built starter home, bijoux studio pad? What price range are you looking at? How much deposit have you saved already? How much do you think you might be able to borrow? The chapter on mortgages will help you devise a strategy to meet that goal.

Similarly if you're saving for a wedding, first baby or school fees how long have you got? How much can you afford to save each month? If you want to quit your job to go travelling, how much do you think you could rent out your home for? How much could you save?

Next to your goals, write down whatever financial dilemmas they pose. Phrase them in the following way: Should I get a fixed or variable rate mortgage? If you want to buy a home abroad in the next five years, 'Should I take out a foreign mortgage, or use equity from my existing home?' If you are expecting a baby you may want to know if you can invest in an ISA on his or her behalf, and what investments to consider.

Giving your CV a makeover

Look carefully at your financial CV and the products in it. Can you spot any more duds in there, as a result of apathy, ignorance or fear, even at this early stage?

Should you change bank accounts? Should you sell your endowment? Should you switch from a technology fund to a more general one? By working through this book, you'll be able to answer a lot of these questions for yourself. You'll also develop the confidence to shop for products you need. However, there are some cases in which you may need professional advice (estate planning, and complicated pensions and investments), so the last chapter gives a full guide to finding a good financial adviser, if you do need one.

3

Financial goddess
of the High Street

This chapter is all about getting the best from your day-to-day
finances. That means earning a good rate of interest when your
current account is in credit and paying the lowest rate possible
when you need to go overdrawn.

It means shunning usurious interest rates on credit and store
cards, but exploiting all their cash-back offers, air miles and
bonus points! It means adding thousands of pounds to your
salary by grabbing every company perk your employer offers
(pensions, company cars, life insurance, season travel loans,
subsidised lunches), and getting the best value on holiday, travel
and car finance.

Shopaholics take note: becoming goddess of the High Street
also means snapping up generous in-store loyalty cards (Boots'
advantage card which gives 4p for every £1 you spend is my
favourite), two-for-one offers and discounts; knowing your consumer rights; not being lured into buying useless extended
warranties; and knowing that you can haggle in designer shops
in Knightsbridge as well as street bazaars in Istanbul!

Financial goddesses know they'll always get better value if they cut out the middle man, so they shop online for their investments, insurances and loans. As they're pretty clued up on money, business and the law, they know how to find a good financial adviser, accountant or solicitor if they need one – and exactly how to make a complaint if they get let down!

Becoming goddess of the High Street will do wonders for your finances – but be warned, everyone from financial advisers to your bank manager will probably begin to hate you, because they won't be able to squeeze more money out of you!

Become mistress of your current account

Of all your financial products, your current account is the one you have everyday contact with, so it's important the two of you get on!

The first step to becoming a financial goddess is to ensure you have the best bank account for your needs. Unfortunately, many of us fail at this first stage – how many times have you heard the refrain: 'I hate my bank!'

What you need from a bank

You need a current account to pay in your salary and cheques, set up direct debits and withdraw cash. If you've got funds sitting in your account, you want to be paid a decent rate of interest on the money you're kindly making available to the bank. If you need to borrow, you want to do so at the most competitive interest rate, and without generating additional charges like 'monthly fees' – what are they for?

You need free and easy access to cash machines at home and abroad, the ability to transfer money between your accounts, and regular statements to keep track of everything.

You don't need or want anything else (ISAs, pensions,

mortgages, insurances, credit cards, gold accounts or financial advice) from your bank, unless they represent genuinely good value.

The Big Four

Britain's 'Big Four' High Street banks – NatWest, Lloyds TSB, Barclays and HSBC, have come in for a lot of flak from the government and consumer organisations, and rightly so.

They wield an enormous amount of power over the nation's finances – 70 per cent of us bank with one of them. But overall, they're a slow, inefficient, expensive bunch. They get away with offering uncompetitive accounts and shoddy service because they know the average Brit has a remarkably apathetic attitude towards changing bank accounts.

It's one of those puzzling human character traits, that we'll happily compose an eloquent eleven-page letter of complaint about our bank to *Watchdog*, but end up 'sticking with the devil we know' rather than going through the rigmarole of changing our lot!

But such apathy is costing us dear. As a nation, we're paying between £3bn and £5bn too much a year for our banking services – that's a cost of between £40 and £400 per household.

How are the Big Four squeezing us?
Typically, they pay less than 1 per cent interest on accounts in credit, compared with online banks (like Cahoot, Zurich Bank and Intelligent Finance) which pay between 3 per cent and 4 per cent – about thirty times more interest over a whole year!

They also charge punitive rates of interest on overdrafts – around 15 per cent to 19 per cent for an authorised overdraft, and anything up to 25 per cent plus charges of up to £5 a day if you dare to slip into the red without asking.

They have also been criticised for the way they calculate interest on their credit cards: while they may advertise a reasonable headline APR rate, they actually use a higher rate to calculate the interest, and you have to be a mathematical genius to figure out how they've done their sums.

So unless there's a very good reason why you are banking with one of the Big Four, think seriously about moving. (If you're a recent graduate you might have negotiated a very low rate loan or overdraft to pay off student debts – if so, take the offer, and move on when it expires!)

Avoid other financial products from the Big Four

You can barely get a cheque stamped at one of the Big Four banks these days without being asked if you'd like to see their 'client relationship manager' or 'have a financial wealth check', or if you'd be interested in buying their 'great value' home or car insurance, perhaps?

One of the biggest axes I have to grind with the Big Four is that they're hell-bent on luring customers into buying a plethora of expensive, poorly managed financial products. And they've become rather good at lulling us into a false sense of security too.

In 2000, Abbey National hooked up with Costa Coffee to create a cosy 'coffee shop and bank' utopia in certain branches. In these open-plan emporiums, you can sip a cappuccino, flick through the day's papers, dump your kids in a creche, and do your banking.

If you're getting a genuinely good deal (and to be fair, at the time of writing, Abbey National was paying 3 per cent interest on accounts in credit), great. If not, pop in for a croissant, but take your banking elsewhere!

The Big Four High Street banks are just that – banks. They are not stockbrokers, fund managers, insurance providers, financial advisers (or coffee shops). Their pensions, ISAs, mortgages and insurances are rarely going to be as good as those offered by specialists, because they simply don't have the expertise to manage them, and have too many middlemen to be competitive (though you can always haggle!).

Just to give you an example of what a rotten deal you'd have got if (through ignorance) you'd bought an ISA from a bank instead of an investment house: in the five years to 2000, the FTSE 100 index rose by 162.34 per cent, yet Barclay's 500 trust only managed to deliver 56.89 per cent growth. By investing with a High Street bank instead of a leading investment house, you are likely to talk yourself out of several thousands of pounds in the long term.

Similarly, when in June 1997, I did a financial makeover for a London chef who had been saving £25 a month into a Barclays' pension for several years, I discovered that all the contributions he had made in the *first two years* had been eaten up in charges, and that the pension fund had been one of the worst performers in its sector.

I'm not picking on Barclays (I've actually got quite a good mortgage from them), I'm simply making the point that, just as you wouldn't expect to find the most chic dinner party ware in Woolworths, you're not going to find the most impressive investments, mortgages and pensions at your High Street bank, either.

And finally: say 'No' to rip-off 'premium' accounts

If you're a professional woman who is clearly going places, and you bank with one of the Big Four, you can bet your bottom dollar that they'll be falling over themselves to 'upgrade' you to a 'premium' or 'gold' account.

This could cost you anything from £6 a month to £150 a year for empty perks like 'free' travel insurance (but only if you buy your holiday with their credit card), commission-free holiday money (which you can get from the Post Office anyway) or a platinum gold credit card (do you really need another one?), and perhaps a 'personal bank manager' who'll remember your birthday.

I know it's nice to think you belong to a 'high-prestige club', but the sad fact is that many of these accounts are actually open to any Tom, Dick or Harry. You'll end up paying more in fees than you would if you'd shopped around for the perks yourself, and have nothing to show for it.

Banks are under huge pressure to increase their profits, hence their foray into the world of 'premium accounts', investments and coffee shops. Personally, I wouldn't pay 60p to see a personal bank manager. So unless you feel the benefits really are worth it, say no.

Why does it take so long for a cheque to clear?

While even the most humble corner shops seem to have embraced basic modern technology with relative ease, Britain's banks are still operating a creaking snail-mail system of clearing cheques, harking back to the Dickensian age. Why it can take up to eight working days for funds deposited by cheque to become available for use is quite beyond me. But here's their explanation.

Banks adopt two dates for clearing cheques. The first – known as 'cleared for value', is the date on which the cheque (having been passed through the bank's clearing system) is debited from the payee's account, shows up on your account, but curiously doesn't actually become available for you to use. Instead it sits in the bank's coffers earning them interest for a couple of days until they feel ready to pass it on to you.

This is the second date, known as the 'cleared for fate' date. With very inefficient banks it can be as much as three days after the first 'cleared for value' date. So, in effect, the bank is 'borrowing' your money, free of charge, to earn interest for themselves.

Of course, if you dare to go overdrawn, your bank will clock up interest the very minute the first pound slips into the red, but they don't seem to have any conscience about using your money for free.

In Australia, banks seem to have got their act together and transmit cheque details electronically. The cheques still have to be physically passed through the clearing system, but at least the process has been speeded up, and funds are usually available for use within three to four days.

I probably don't need to add that if you're paying in a foreign cheque at your British bank, it can take several weeks to clear. That's because the cheque needs to be sent to the payee's country and, despite major advances in overseas travel, it still takes British banks several weeks to do that.

Changing bank accounts has never been easier (I did it!)

The good news is that switching bank accounts has never been easier. Many banks offer 'switcher packs', so they take over the hassle of transferring all your direct debits and salary payments from your old account to your new one.

I finally lost patience and closed my current account with NatWest last summer when they managed to lose my advance cheque for this book, after I'd paid it in through the 'paying-in' service at the ATM machine.

When the money failed to show up on my account seven days later, I went in to investigate. Half an hour later, the sheepish-looking branch manager suggested by way of explanation that as they had 'so many cheques passing through their system' they might simply have 'thrown mine away' – just like that! Charming.

She promised that I would be 'adequately compensated'. Two weeks later, a lifeless-looking bunch of flowers was delivered to my door, followed by a three-line letter saying that as the bank had been 'unable to determine' exactly what had happened, would I 'please accept their sincere apologies'.

If I'd lost a significant amount of money belonging to someone else, I'd have launched an investigation and compensated the victim financially for the inconvenience and financial loss of having to get the cheque replaced, not fobbed them off with flowers.

I now bank online with Cahoot and, joy of joys, will never have to go into a bank again. I can log onto my computer and check my statement at any time of day or night, and the first cheque I paid into my account cleared within two working days.

There have been one or two high-profile security breaches with online bank accounts (just as there have with the Inland Revenue's online self-assessment system). But by and large, it's pretty safe provided you choose a secure system, identifiable by a closed padlock symbol at the bottom right hand of your screen. Most banks use 128-bit encryption software, one of the highest level civilian systems available – and are unlikely to let cheques go astray!

A goddess' best friend is her credit card

Once upon a time, we did all our shopping with cash and the occasional cheque. Today, plastic is fantastic – in America, it's considered almost vulgar to actually have cash on you.

Credit cards are great – they're convenient, streetwise, and offer protection. If you buy an item worth more than £100 with a credit card and it proves to be faulty, both the trader and the credit card provider are liable, and you can demand a refund from the latter.

This also applies to goods purchased abroad, though you may have to battle with some credit card providers to get them to recognise the fact. In any case, when you are travelling you should always carry an internationally recognised card like Visa or Mastercard (preferably both).

A double-edged sword

But credit cards are a double-edged sword. If you pay them off each month, so never accrue a penny interest, but take advantage of all the incentives, they're a girl's best friend. But, if you pay off just the minimum balance (or pay late), they become an ugly debt monster.

Building up debts on credit cards (or even worse, store cards), is the most expensive form of borrowing, as the interest charged is typically double that of low-cost loans, and can be more than five times that of a typical mortgage.

If you have debts outstanding on several credit cards, scour the best buys tables in the newspapers for the cheapest loan or overdraft and consolidate all your debts onto one of them. Then devise a budget to pay this off as soon as possible. More on this in the next chapter.

Once again: cash is queen

As we said right at the beginning: cash is queen. Repeat this to yourself each and every time you step out of the door to embark on a shopping trip, because it's very easy to forget in today's dangerous new world of easy credit.

When a financial goddess wants something, she *saves* for it, (or as a very last resort borrows at the cheapest rate possible). She does not succumb to the titillation of 'buy now, pay later' and become what Michael Gove, writing in *The Times* in November 2002, dubbed 'capitalists without capital'.

Zero per cent credit cards

There are nearly 1500 credit cards to choose from in Britain today. You may have spotted cards offering an introductory 0 per cent APR (the amount of interest you pay over a year on the money you borrow). This is just what it says – an introductory offer, which usually lasts for no more than six months, after which the rate soars to anything up to 19 per cent. If you only need credit for a few months, and are sure you'll clear the bill in full before the standard rate kicks in, grab the 0 per cent offer by all means. But if you're going to end up paying the higher rate anyway, look for a card which has a consistently low APR instead.

Charity credit cards

Credit card firms offer free airmiles, petrol, cashback or vouchers. Some will also make charitable donations. This is one way of giving money away to charity for free.

There are cards which support cancer and heart foundations, animal and wildlife organisations, arts organisations and even universities. They're called 'affinity cards'. For every pound you spend, the credit card provider will donate a small percentage to the 'affinity' charity. It's a good way of supporting your favourite cause, and if you don't pay interest, it won't cost you a penny.

Keep an eye on your friend – and the fraudsters at bay

Best friends need looking after, and so does your credit card. Credit card fraud is on the increase, having risen from £188m in 1999, to nearly £300m in 2001.

Fraud at ATM machines

Be wary of anyone who offers help if you get into difficulties at a cashpoint – particularly abroad. Card criminals can put a strip of foil into the ATM so when you insert your card, it gets stuck. The crook then steps in to help, persuades you to re-enter your pin number (which they memorise), but of course no joy, so you walk away to report your card is stuck.

Meanwhile, they remove the jam, retrieve your stuck card, stick it in again, punch in your pin number and withdraw oodles of cash – often at several different cashpoints, in the space of minutes.

Counterfeit cards

The other type of fraudster becoming increasingly prevalent is the one who counterfeits your details onto a blank card and then goes on a spending spree. The most dangerous thing about this type of fraud is that you're unlikely to be aware of it until you receive your statement.

Counterfeiting often happens in busy bars and restaurants, where waiters have magnetic strips which 'read' card details on the inside of their aprons. It's always best to pay for meals with cash, and buy drinks individually instead of leaving your card behind the bar.

Avoid giving out your credit card or bank details over the phone to unknown retailers, as they can easily jot down your details. If you're buying over the Internet, ensure it's from a site that has a secure padlock sign in the bottom right-hand corner.

Shopping on a secure Internet site is actually one of the safest ways of using your card as the numbers are immediately scrambled, and even the most sophisticated hacker would have difficulty tapping into them.

Inform your credit card company immediately

If your card is retained at a cashpoint, or gets lost or stolen, inform your bank immediately. The banking code of practice states that unless they can prove gross negligence on your part, you should get your money back.

Credit card companies have all kinds of sophisticated software to pick up on abnormal usage of your card, and may well contact you if they suspect fraud has taken place. Mine did last year when a fraudster ran up hundreds of pounds on videos and petrol amongst other things, and I don't run a car.

Finally, if you screw up till receipts and leave them in the little bins at the end of the supermarket checkout, beware. There's even a breed of card fraudsters who scour bins for lurking credit card details – sad but true.

The shopping goddess

Now for some real girl power. Learn to shop like a goddess, and not only will you become the undisputed subject of admiration among friends, you'll also save yourself loads of money.

The four key areas to master are: knowing your consumer rights, learning to haggle, getting best value travel and car finance, and becoming a financial e-chick.

Your consumer rights

When you buy an item or service, you have a right to expect it to be a) in perfect working condition (unless a soil or defect was marked at the time of purchase), b) fit for its purpose, and c) exactly as it was described (even if it's second-hand, or in the sale). If an item fails to satisfy these criteria, you're entitled to a full refund.

When you buy an item from a shop, you enter into a contract with the vendor, so they have to take full responsibility for the item they're selling, and cannot fob you off by saying it's 'the manufacturer's fault'. You don't have to accept a credit note or a replacement for goods that are faulty or not what they purported to be. And you don't legally have to show a receipt, though it's always a good idea.

Faulty goods should be returned as soon as possible, though vendors are legally liable for them for six years! You may also be able to claim compensation for faulty goods. So if a defective iron burns a hole in your blouse ask for the shop manager and see if they can compensate you for the cost of a replacement.

Distance shopping

If you buy something over the Internet, or through mail order or a TV channel, it's known as distance shopping and you have the right to cancel, for any reason, within seven days. You're also entitled to a full refund if goods do not arrive on time.

Similarly, if a service is not provided on time – say your dry cleaning is late – ask for a discount. If you unwittingly make a purchase from an unsolicited salesperson in your own home, you have a seven-day cooling off period, in which to change your mind.

Charm your way into getting a discount

One of the most instructive journalistic assignments I ever carried out, was going round lots of shops in London asking for a discount on everything from antique furniture to handbags, designer clothes and paintings.

My father has always been a good haggler. I remember how he once charmed his way into getting a discount on a new sofa with such skill the poor shop owner joked perhaps he should write 'nearly paid' on the receipt!

But I'd never thought of doing it myself – till then. Perhaps it was just luck that I managed to get a further 15 per cent knocked off a Gucci jacket in the sale that first day. In fact every shop I went into (five in all, from clothes to antique shops), when I took an item up to the cashier and asked for a discount, they said 'Yes'. Sadly, the assignment didn't come with the cash to buy the goods!

Shops will often knock 10 to 15 per cent off the marked price of goods they're eager to get rid off, particularly during the sales, when they're keen to clear their floors to make way for new collections, so any price is better than none. I bought an 'end of the range' bed off the shop floor for half price the week before I moved into my first home.

Electrical stores will almost always 'match' the best price on the High Street, and 'throw in' free blank videos, disks, leads, etc. (never pay for batteries). The magic words 'I'm a loyal customer' should get you at least 10 per cent knocked off furniture and white goods. Hotels all over the world will slash their rates on empty rooms late in the day. And you'd be daft ever to pay the full asking price for an oil painting, Indian rug or antique piece – these people *expect* you to haggle.

So don't save your bargaining skills for exotic holidays, make it second nature, like saving and investing. After all, shops aren't embarrassed about putting a 100 per cent mark-up on goods!

Travel shopping

I'm intrigued to know how certain author friends have perfected the art of getting upgraded to business class each time they fly. (I once interviewed a teddy bear collector, who told me that checking onto a flight with a designer teddy bear in your arm is the surest way of getting upgraded!)

If you're travelling on business or fly frequently with the same airline, but don't happen to have a stuffed pooch, it might be worth asking for an upgrade. If you're backpacking, don't bother.

Euro shopping

The introduction of the euro has brought mixed responses. Whilst it is undoubtedly simpler to be able to use the same currency across Germany, France, Italy and Spain, it has also led to inflationary 'price convergence' across the euro zone, which has highlighted the fact that prices in Britain really are a rip off. In fact they're almost 13 per cent higher than the average euro price.

A survey conducted by Dresdner Kleinwort Wassertein, an investment bank, found that a bottle of Coca Cola in London cost €1.92, but just €0.17 in Paris, €1.45 in Amsterdam and €1.90 in Frankfurt. It also concluded that some of the greatest price differentials were in taxi rides. These varied from €0.70 (45p) per km in Rome to €3 (£1.90) in Brussels. The other service for which there was a wide disparity was hairdressers: the cost of getting a haircut ranged from € 21 (£13.39) in Madrid to €49.73 (£31.70) in Paris.

So the message seems to be: don't get your hair cut in Paris, and avoid taxis in Brussels!

Goddess guide to car finance

While property tends to appreciate in value, cars depreciate. A survey by *Which?* found that some modern cars lose more than three-quarters of their value in the first three years. This makes it all the more important that you don't get ripped off with an expensive car finance package when buying a flash new set of wheels. If you need to borrow, take out a cheap loan.

The cheapest way to borrow money to buy a car is an everyday low-cost loan and, again, the best deals will be found on the Internet. In August 2002, a three-year finance deal with Peugeot would boost the total cost of a 206 model from £10,595 to £13,926. But by picking out the best loan available on moneysupermarkets.co.uk (7.1 per cent) the total you would pay would be £11,623, giving you a saving of £2,303.

Buy your car online
You can also save yourself thousands of pounds by buying your car through the net. A growing army of British drivers are shunning UK car dealers in favour of online dealers like Virgin, Eurekar and Oneswoop, which can save them more than 10 per cent on the list price of a new model by buying through a European importer. Carpricecheck.co.uk is a website that monitors the price of thousands of models available through

car makers, dealers and importers and says that one in twenty UK drivers now buys their car online.

And, although women apparently lack the special awareness skills of men, which means they are worse at reversing into tight car parking spaces, they are on the whole perceived to be safe drivers, which means they get a better deal on car insurance too.

Become a financial e-chick

Most twenty and thirtysomethings are pretty au fait with the joys of surfing the Internet for everything from books, to designer handbags and last minute flights.

When the Prudential launched Egg, its Internet bank, in 1998, it revolutionised the savings market with high-interest deposit accounts and other banks soon followed suit. Today, the smart financial goddess knows running her finances online will save her time and paperwork, but also money.

Because online providers deal direct with customers on their computers, they don't have to pay third-party salespeople commission or fund and staff High Street branches, so they can pass on the savings they make to you.

We explained above how online current accounts offer a far better deal than branch accounts. The chapter on investments illustrates how you can make huge savings by shopping online for your ISAs. You can also save yourself hundreds of pounds in interest by shopping online for your mortgage and insurance. In fact, some of the greatest savings to be had online are on car and home insurance.

Direct Line automatically gives car drivers a 5 per cent discount for purchasing their insurance online, and you can save up to two-thirds of the cost of home insurance by comparing deals on the net. You can pick up bestselling books for half price on Amazon.co.uk; and the increasing number of

British drivers importing cheaper cars from Europe over the net has forced UK dealers to cut their prices too.

Employee benefits

Far too many women underestimate the value of the perks their company offers, simply because they are not aware of them. Although the days of a job for life are long gone, pension contributions, life cover, long-term sick pay and health insurance mean a £25,000 salary could actually be worth £32,000.

Many companies have closed their final-salary pension schemes to new entrants, but will still contribute a percentage of your salary to a pension. As the chapter on pensions illustrates, building up a retirement fund is an expensive business, and this is money for free, so you should take it.

Some companies which do not run final-salary pensions offer income replacement insurance, which, like a final salary pension, would pay out a monthly income until you retire, if you contracted a long-term illness which prevented you from working. Employers can purchase this form of insurance quite cheaply, but buying £1,000 a month of income insurance privately could cost you more than £700 a year.

Given Britain's creaking National Health Service, quick and easy access to private medical care is also an attractive perk which many companies offer. Although you are taxed on the medical premiums your employer makes on your behalf, this will still be just a fraction of what it would cost you to buy health insurance independently.

If you have dependents, you should certainly take advantage of any life cover your employer offers. This would pay a tax-free lump sum of up to four times your salary in the event of your death.

Single women do not need life cover. However, they may be

able to negotiate another benefit instead. Many companies offer flexible benefits packages, so you can spend, say, 3 per cent of your salary on perks of your choice like childcare, dental care, extra holidays or simply cash.

If you are thinking of changing jobs to an employer who offers fewer perks but a higher salary, it may well be worth contacting a financial adviser specialising in employee benefits to calculate the true worth of the package. If the 'pay rise' actually means you are worse off in terms of benefits, it may give you ammunition to negotiate an even better pay rise.

4

Cash is queen: savings and debts

Saving is a primary financial skill. Having a rainy day fund put by will not only give you financial security, but also psychological comfort too.

Saving is also the first rung of the investment pyramid. Because stockmarket investments carry risks, you cannot afford to start investing until you have built up a defensive layer of cash savings to cushion you in the event of a stockmarket dip. And you cannot begin saving until you have cleared all your debts. So even if you owe just a few hundred pounds on your overdraft, start clearing it today.

Unfortunately, debt has become such a way of life for many people today, that far too many of us have just become immune to the fact that we are living off borrowed money.

It is inevitable that students today will start their working lives several thousands of pounds in debt. And if there is an upside to this, it is that having had to manage debt early on, they will be better equipped psychologically to deal with more complex financial planning issues in later years.

'Good' debts and 'bad' debts

Student debt is certainly a worry for most twentysomethings, but low-cost loans and overdrafts used for tuition fees, books, rent and other essentials needed to get to graduation are not necessarily 'bad' debts.

For those who pass with good results and make the most of their time at college, a university education will pay lifetime dividends in the form of a better paid or more rewarding job than if they'd gone straight to work after school.

Most of us have to borrow many tens of thousands of pounds to purchase our homes, and rightly regard it as an investment. In short, if the purpose of taking on a debt is to achieve one of your financial goals, and it is planned and managed properly, it is not something to be feared.

Debt turns into a nasty four-letter word when it is unplanned, uncontrolled and unaccountable. For example, when a student who has already taken out £5,000 in loans to pay her tuition fees and rent, then takes out another three or four credit cards to buy clothes, furniture, holidays, meals out and computers, thinking she'll just pay it all off when she graduates and gets a job. Few graduates earn more than £20,000 in their first year (and they're the lucky ones). If she walked out of college with £30,000 debts, she could be paying them off till she's forty-five.

Bad debt is when you let your current account keep slipping unwittingly into the red, but instead of paying it off as soon as you can, you just ignore it so the hole gets bigger. It's when you fail to adjust your spending patterns after downsizing to a lower paid job or starting a family. Or when you jump on the 'buy now, pay later' bandwagon, and never catch up.

We're presented with myriad opportunities to fall into the debt trap, when we should actually be *saving more* for our future.

It may be some years before today's 'live for today at the

expense of tomorrow', timebomb explodes, but when it does, it's going to be a nasty shock. So if you're teetering on the brink of a vicious debt trap, this is your wake-up call. Get a grip now before you pull yourself into the downward lifetime spiral of snakes and ladders.

If you're already drowning in a sea of debt, take a deep breath and read on. With a clear head and a five-point plan, you can get your finances back on track quicker than you think.

Managing debt like a goddess

As we said, you can't start achieving financial dreams until you've got out of debt, so even if you owe just a few hundred pounds, tackle the monster now.

Building wealth is like constructing a pyramid: you need a thick, wide foundation to reach for the six-figure lump sum. If you've got debts, you've got a hole in your ground, and if you don't fill it first, all the savings and investments you pile on top will just fall through! Below are two step-by-step approaches to getting rid of your debts for good.

The first is aimed at cappuccino goddesses starting their working lives hungover with student debts. The second is for those who have accumulated piles and piles of consumer debts on the back of overdrafts, loans, credit cards and mortgages.

Five-point plan to clearing debt for the graduate goddess

Only the lucky few have a well-paid job lined up the summer they leave university. Finding your ideal job may take a few years, and you have to weigh up whether it's worth taking up any job (even if it doesn't make use of your degree) to pay the bills and start paying off some of your student debts, or doing voluntary work or further training, to break into your desired field.

1. Unless you're earning less than £833 per month, repayments on student loans begin the April after graduation and are collected by the Inland Revenue, through the PAYE scheme or self-assessment. You pay 9 per cent of your salary in excess of £10,000 in monthly instalments so as your salary rises, so do your repayments. Interest is charged at the rate of inflation (currently hovering between 2 and 2.5 per cent) so this is one of the cheapest forms of borrowing you're ever likely to get.

   You can make overpayments on your student loan if you like, and if it's the only debt you have, you may as well. But most students have overdrafts and bank loans as well, which will be costing a hell of a lot more in interest, so these should be tackled first.

2. If you have bank loans and overdrafts, ask your bank manager if they can tailor a competitive 'graduate banking package' with a cheap (or free) overdraft and bank loan facility for you. At the time of writing, Lloyds TSB was offering graduates an interest-free overdraft of up to £2000 for three years.

3. Any borrowing over £2000 should be converted into a loan, as this will be cheaper and easier to manage than an overdraft. (Again, at the time of writing Abbey National was offering a maximum £5000 loan to be repaid over three years at just 3 per cent, provided you apply within six months of graduating.) As a potential high-earning professional, banks will want your custom, so negotiate the best package you can for yourself.

4. Be realistic: if your outgoings and debts are preventing you from having a social life, and finding a worthwhile job is proving tough, perhaps it's worth moving back home

instead of wasting money on rent? Employers are fully aware of the debts new graduates face, so if you do land a good job, ask if they can help out by perhaps offering an interest-free travel loan or, if the job takes you to a different part of the country, with relocation costs.

5. It's not just books, essays and exams you leave behind when you graduate from university. You'll also be kissing goodbye to student discounts on everything from beer and clothes to cinema tickets and stationery. This comes as a shock to many new graduates, so adjust your spending and social life according to the cost of living in the real world.

Capitalists without capital: give up playing snakes and ladders with debt

In November 2002, Michael Gove of *The Times* wrote how his income has never caught up with his heroic spending, saying: 'It's a sad fact of human existence that once you start living beyond your means you carry on doing so, and even as your means grow to allow you to live within them perfectly happily, your expenditure still carries on outstripping current resources.' He dubbed such people 'capitalists without capital'.

If you're borrowing money today in the hope that you'll earn it back tomorrow, you fall into this camp, and no matter how talented and well paid you are at the moment, you're in danger of never catching up with your debts. Instead of building a solid pyramid of savings and investments, you'll be forever playing the 'snakes and ladders' game of debt, creeping up slowly into credit every now and then, but slithering back into the red with twice the speed!

If this sounds familiar, you need to tackle your psychological attitude to spending, and pull yourself back up onto the straight and narrow. Follow the three-step plan below.

1. Cash is queen

Repeat the mantra *cash is queen* over and over again because until it sinks in and you rid yourself of the notion of shopping off credit, you're never going to cure yourself of debt.

Cut up all your credit cards, and put away your cheque book and debit cards. From now on, the only shopping tools at your disposal are good old-fashioned notes and coins.

Next Sunday, draw up a budget of how much you'll need for groceries, travel costs, lunches, household expenses, etc, for the week. Go to the cash machine and withdraw no more than that amount. The £80, £100 or £150 you withdrew is *all* you have to spend for the next seven days. Keep a *diary* of where your money goes for a month.

It's far too easy to 'forget' that you're actually spending when you put everything onto plastic. But when you have to physically part with £10, £20 or £50 notes each time something takes your fancy, or a friend suggests going for an impromptu dinner or film, it seems a lot more real. It's then that you realise that frittering away £88 on six books, a scented candle, some new moisturiser, a packet of ready-to-eat chicken fillets and a tub of Häagen-Dazs, when you just popped out to get some sellotape, really is a bit profligate!

As you jot down your expenses at the end of each day, identify ways of cutting the weekly bill. Perhaps you could find a cheaper hair conditioner, or take a delicious homemade pasta salad into work for lunch a couple of times a week instead of going off to the local gastro-pub.

You should aim to trim at least 15 per cent off your weekly bill, and put this towards clearing your debts. If this sounds painful, remember, the larger your debts and the longer you take to repay them, the more it will cost you in interest, and the less you'll have to spend in the long term.

2. Maintain your palace

Next, prioritise your expenses. As we said in the first chapter, a goddess' home is her palace, so keeping up with mortgage or rent payments, council tax and utility bills is absolutely essential.

You can go without a mobile phone for a few months, but not without gas or water. If you're having trouble paying your mortgage, talk to your lender immediately. They may suggest extending the term of your mortgage, which would reduce your monthly payments. The last thing they want to do is repossess your house. But if you start missing payments without explanation, they'll assume the worst, and get heavy.

Don't borrow more to pay off debts. *Never* borrow money to pay off another debt: owing several pots of money to different banks and credit cards at different rates of interest and on different days of the month is confusing, and will have you spinning around in circles.

Cancel non-essential direct debits like gym memberships, pension payments, regular savings into investments, union or club memberships (you can restart the investment plans when you're back on an even keel, but there's no point in saving when you've got debts around your neck).

Do not cancel life insurance if you've got dependants, or home insurance if you're a homeowner. It's just not worth the risk. Instead shop around for cheaper policies.

Contact the Citizens Advice Bureau to see if you are entitled to any tax credits or benefits (like child tax credit, working family tax credit or unemployment benefit) and how to claim them. And finally, but most importantly: Look the monster in the face. Get out all your credit card statements, bills, overdraft letters and lay them out on a clean table. Add them all up, and calculate how much you can reasonably afford to pay off each month. You may have bills you have left unopened; take a deep breath and open them now. Set aside one hour each week, when you will simply file away all your bills and review your debt clearing progress.

Burying your head in the sand is the most dangerous (though most natural) thing you can do when you are in debt. The debts will just mount up, and you'll be charged more interest and eventually get threatening letters and demands, which may end up costing you twice as much as if you'd paid them off in the first place. That's the real monster of debt!

3. Consolidate your debts – but *never* use a 'debt consolidation' service

Because paying off debt is expensive, the most efficient way of doing so is to consolidate everything onto the lowest rate possible. But don't even think of resorting to 'debt consolidation services' frequently advertised in newspapers.

And don't take out a loan using your home as security either – it's as risky as it sounds. 'Debt consolidators' are unregulated. If they claim to offer a counselling service or to be insolvency practitioners, they're likely to be unqualified and unscrupulous. They'll charge fees for their services, levy ridiculously high rates of interest, and persecute you when you fail to meet their demands.

If you're many thousands of pounds in debt and have equity in your home, consider adding the debts to your mortgage, or extending the mortgage term. You'll pay a much lower rate of interest on a good mortgage than you would on a loan, but as the repayments will be stretched out over several years, you'll have paid more over the long term.

If you're thinking of increasing your mortgage, now is a good opportunity to remortgage – particularly if you've been throwing away thousands of pounds a year on the variable rate. But before rushing to apply for a bigger mortgage, be sure you can afford the new repayments, both at the current rate *and* if interest rates rise *by 2 per cent.*

At the time of writing interest rates are at their lowest for forty years, but they will rise again when economic conditions improve, and your repayments will shoot up with them.

If you're looking to increase your mortgage, don't be afraid to bargain with your lender if you think the rate they are offering is uncompetitive – you're a goddess of the High Street, remember!

Debtbuster: how to clear £1000–£30,000 debts

If you've got money owing on cards, loans and overdrafts, tot it all up, and consolidate as follows. If the amount comes to:

- between £250 and £1000 and you can pay it off in less than six months, find a bank which offers the cheapest overdraft. The best ones will automatically offer an interest-free buffer zone up to £250, anyway.
- between £1001 and £15,000, it could take anything from six months to a few years to get rid of this, so scour the best-buy tables in the newspapers and apply for the cheapest flexible loan. 'Flexible' means you can pay off the full amount at any time without incurring a penalty, so if you do get a windfall, or your income comes in periodic lump sums, you can clear the debt in one clean sweep!
- anything over £15,000 and you have equity in your home, adding all your debts to your mortgage might be the most efficient way of paying it off, providing you can afford the new repayments, even if rates go up. If not, scout around for the cheapest low-cost loan.

The more you borrow, the lower the rate will be. As I said, it's far better to owe one big sum to a single lender than have two or three little loans from different lenders. That way you'll always know exactly where you are, and how much progress you're making paying it off.

You're also more likely to face up to the debt if you've got one big sum staring you in the face rather than several confusing little ones which might trick you into conviniently forgetting about some of them!

Credit ratings

Big Brother is watching: do you know your credit rating?

Did you know that your finances are being watched like a hawk? In Britain, two credit reference agencies, Experian and Equifax, hold credit files on the vast majority of us.

Before giving credit, lenders will contact one of them to ensure you are credit worthy. Defaulting on credit payments and bills could affect your credit rating, and make it difficult for you to obtain a mortgage, loan, or even a store card in the future – another reason not to let your finances get out of control.

The points system

Credit files work on a points system. If you are an employed homeowner over the age of twenty-five, registered on the electoral role, with a telephone in your own name, and a clean credit record, you'll score more highly that a twenty-year-old casual worker moving from one shared house to another, with no credit history.

Being on the electoral register is very important for your financial respectability, so if you're moving from one flat to another, make sure you update your local council each time you move.

What to do if you've been turned down for credit

If you've been turned down for credit, write to one of the agencies, with details of your addresses over the past three years, plus a cheque for £2. They are obliged to reply within seven days, and amend your file (or make a note that a particular entry has been challenged) and to pass on the information to the credit lender who made the search on you.

Sometimes, there can be mix-ups if the previous occupier at your address had a similar sounding name to yours and a bad credit record.

Also, if you'd had a disagreement with a mobile phone or utilities company over a bill, they may have lodged this on your credit file. Explain this to the credit agency and they should amend your file accordingly.

If you have had any county court judgments for defaulting on payments, they will remain on your credit file for six years, and you will most certainly have difficulty obtaining a mortgage from a High Street lender.

Unclaimed windfalls

If this is all starting to sound a bit depressing, take heart from this: there's about £15.3bn in life assurance policies, premium bond prizes, dormant bank accounts, investments and lottery money sitting in Britain's coffers waiting to be claimed! Some of it could be for you!

If your parents bought you premium bonds which you've forgotten about, or you opened a building society savings account as a child, or just bought an investment many years ago, it might be worth checking if money is owed to you. In 1999, 17.7m of premium bond prizes were registered as unclaimed – one of them for £25,000!

There's no time limit for retrieving prizes, and you can check if you're a winner on the National Savings' website. You'll need your premium bond numbers, so if you've lost them write to National Savings with your full name, any previous names and all addresses. Since premium bonds were launched over forty years ago, nearly 99 per cent of winners have eventually been traced.

If you opened a savings account as a child or student, and the bank has not been able to make contact with you, the account will have been made 'dormant'. To trace it, you'll need to fill in a form available from most bank branches, or contact the British Bankers' Association.

If you have a parent or relative who recently passed away, you might be entitled to some of their estate. There's about £500,000 lying in unclaimed life assurance policies. Often this is because policyholders change address but fail to inform their insurer, so there's no way of matching the money to its rightful owner, and the money just builds up. If you think you may have money due to you from a deceased parent, relative or partner, it might be worth checking the Unclaimed Assets Register (all contact details and addresses can be found in the appendix) for a small fee.

One of the most heartwarming stories I ever wrote was on a live-in nanny in her early sixties who received a call from Standard Life in January 2000 to say a cheque for £30,000 from a matured endowment policy was on its way to her! She had taken out the policy when she bought her family home in Cumbria in 1974, then moved to London to work as a nurse, but never told the insurance firm of her new address. Standard Life managed to trace her through the UK Central Council for Nursing and Midwifery, twenty-six years later!

Saving

Finding the money to save today

So now you've cleared your debts, it's time to start building wealth. As we said at the beginning, the first step to building wealth is *saving*.

Financial goddesses are not zealots. They get a kick out of saving, but they realise the main purpose of doing so is to create more money to *spend*.

Saving is not a pointless academic exercise in stashing away every last penny and living a miserly life, it's about creating a richer life. So the fully-fledged financial goddess is both a *saver* and a *spender*.

Look at your spending diet

But have you ever marvelled at how some women always seem to have the money to buy clothes, eat out, go the theatre, have a holiday, pay their mortgage and stay out of debt, while earning less than you? Do you wonder how on earth they can get away with spending so much, on so little?

Well, I don't know a heck of a lot about dieting, but I have heard it said that when an overweight person complains that he eats 'less' than his trimmer friends but still can't lose weight, what he really means is that he is eating less of the 'wrong foods'. As I say, I can't comment on that, but what I can say is that roughly the same theory does apply to our personal finances.

If you fill your shopping basket with stylish ready-made meals, exotic salads, fancy breads and luscious desserts at the supermarket each week; always take short taxi rides instead of walking; pick up a cappuccino and panini while waiting for your partner at the station; buy a lipstick and pair of shoes in the sales, drop in for a manicure in your lunch hour, and pick up three magazines at the station on your way home from work, your overdraft will quickly become obese!

On the other hand, if you treat yourself and your partner to a really nice bottle of wine a couple of times a week, only take a cab when you're really in a rush (or it's raining), and save that sweater for when you get your pay cheque at the end of the month, you're hardly being parsimonious, but your bank balance will stay quite trim.

So if you're finding it difficult to save, scrutinise your spending diet. Are you a go-for-broke carbohydrate-seeker constantly piling on the pounds with meals out, weekends away, new clothes and shoes you've never even taken out of their shiny bags? Are you an occasional splurger who goes on wild spending sprees every now and then? Are you a spending bulimic who shops till she drops, then feels so guilty that she needs to go shopping all over again to ease her conscience? Or are you a 'balanced eater' who spends in moderation and therefore always has a few pounds left over at the end of the month – a true financial goddess?

You might not be able to change your body image, but you *can* control the shape of your bank account. Gorging on every treat in sight will have your overdraft bulging at the seams, but a little of what you fancy in moderation, won't do you any harm at all.

Saving means paying yourself first

Still not convinced? Listen to this. In the bestselling fable *The Richest Man in Babylon*, Arkad, the eponymous 'rich man', says to his eager disciple: 'I found the road to wealth when I decided that a part of all I earned was mine to keep . . . Do you not pay the garment-maker? Do you not pay the sandal-maker? Do you not pay for the things you eat? You fool. You pay everyone but yourself. You labour for others.'

Exactly! By spending every penny you have and keeping nothing back for yourself, you are simply labouring away for the benefit of the All Bar Ones, Marks & Spencers, French Connections, River Islands, Our Prices and Clinton Cards of this world.

You may be buying yourself instant gratification, but in doing so you are lining the pockets of others, rather than yourself. You're working hard and throwing your money away. In short, you are living for today at the expense of tomorrow, and using your hard-earned money to pay everyone else except yourself. So stop labouring for others and start paying yourself today.

How much should you save?

How much should you save – £25 a month, £50 a month, £100 a month? As we said at the beginning of the chapter, savings are essentially 'rainy day funds' or 'insurance money'; they're not investments that are going to create wealth.

Ideally you need savings equivalent to three months' salary, which you can dip into should you lose your job, need to get your car or boiler fixed, or need emergency medical treatment. The rule of thumb is to aim to be putting aside at least 10 to 15 per cent of your take-home pay into saving and investments.

If you're self-employed, you should automatically be putting away 25 per cent of all your earnings into a cash ISA or high-interest savings account for your tax bills. The best way to save is by monthly direct debit. This way the money is automatically paid into your savings account, just like your council tax and mortgage are paid to your bank and local council, without you having to make a conscious effort. This way you really are *paying* yourself.

Why it is harder to save in Britain today

But I agree it's not easy. Rising house prices, soaring transport costs and plunging stockmarkets are only the half of it. We're not called 'rip-off Britain' for nothing.

British employees work longer hours than their German, French, Italian and Spanish counterparts, pay more taxes (about 13 per cent of our total income, compared with 10 per cent in Germany and 7 per cent in Spain) and endure a higher cost of living, so it's hardly surprising that Brits save less than their European neighbours. While German women manage to save 15.1 per cent of their income, and the French 15.8 per cent, the average British woman only squirrels away 5 per cent of her disposable income.

Add to this the lousy weather, and no wonder 60 per cent of people in a survey said they would emigrate if they got the chance!

Cash ISAs

So now you've found the money to save, where should you put it? Banks and building societies offer savings accounts, but most of them are a complete waste of time, because the interest rates they pay are puny.

Online banks offer slightly better rates. However, the best place for your rainy day funds is a *cash ISA* (individual savings account), which allows you to keep all the *interest* you earn on your account, *tax free*.

There are two types of ISAs:

- *cash ISAs*, which are similar to building society savings accounts except that you don't have to pay tax on the interest.
- *equity ISAs*, in which your money is invested in the stockmarket.

We'll be hearing more about equity ISAs in the next chapter. The thing to grasp about them here is that they come as *mini ISAs* and *maxi ISAs*, whereas cash ISAs *only* come as *minis*.

The maximum you can put into *mini ISAs* (cash or equities) is £3000 a year – and you can only have *one of each* in any tax year.

If you're a first-time investor, I would suggest that you take out one mini *cash ISA* and one mini *equity ISA*, until you have sufficient savings put by (three months' salary).

Having built up a sufficient rainy-day reserve, you can start directing much more of your spare cash into a maxi equity ISA, which will make your money grow even more.

You can put up to £7000 into a maxi equity ISA (and if you get a big bonus or inheritance, this would be a good thing to do). However, you would then have to put your cash savings for that tax year into an ordinary savings or deposit account, as you *cannot* hold a maxi and a mini ISA in any one tax year.

How savings grow

Each time the Bank of England decides to lower its interest rate we hear the refrain: 'Good news for borrowers, but bad news for savers.'

It's true, you won't get brilliant returns on your cash savings at the moment – the Bank of England base rate has been at 4 per cent since November 2001, which is great for mortgage payers, but not so good for cash savers.

Indeed, economists fear that it is the low cost of borrowing combined with the super-buoyant housing market, that is spurring an unprecedented number of cash-strapped home-owners to take equity from their home by increasing their mortgages to buy cars, holidays, clothes. If you have a lot of equity in your home, and really need the money, it certainly makes financial sense to borrow this way.

But low interest rates are *not* an excuse *not* to save (or to borrow more). As we said earlier, savings are vital *insurance policies*, that will offer a soft landing in the event of a hard financial blow. They're never going to make you rich like stocks and shares may, but still, a little can go a long way, once you get into the habit of *saving regularly*.

Save through direct debits

The best way to save (and invest) is through *monthly direct debits*. So even if you've only got £50 a month to spare, scour the best-buy tables for the most competitive cash ISA account (at the time of writing it was Northern Rock paying 4.85 per cent), fill in the direct debit form, and start saving until you've built up at least *three months' salary*.

If you put £50 a month into the Northern Rock ISA, you'd have built up £1932 in three years or £3375 in five years (assuming, of course, that the rate doesn't change).

As our rich man of Babylon says: 'Wealth, like a tree, grows from a tiny seed. The first copper you save is the seed from which your tree of wealth shall grow. The sooner you plant that seed, the sooner shall the tree grow, and the more faithfully you nourish and water that tree with consistent savings, the sooner may you bask in contentment beneath its shade.' So get planting.

When to stop saving and start investing

After saving through monthly direct debits for a couple of years you should have built up a modest tax-free sum. More importantly, you'll also have acquired the habit of regular savings – or *paying yourself first*.

Once you've built up at least three months' salary in cash, you have sufficient rainy day funds and it's time to stop saving and start *investing*. Investments are the vehicles that will make your money *grow*.

If you keep all your money in cash and never invest in the stockmarket, you'll never create the wealth you deserve. With stockmarkets around the world having been depressed for the past eighteen months, we all know that stockmarket investments carry risk (sometimes very painful ones). But investing is an art, and even in a depressed market the clever investment goddess can make her money grow.

The next chapter will show you how to build an investment pyramid, starting with a 'safety first' £1000 investment, and building up to a Rolls Royce tax-free portfolio.

Investments are what will help us achieve our ultimate financial goals. House in France, new sports car, school fees, round the world holiday? It's never going to happen if you keep your money stuffed under the mattress, so read on.

5

Investing like a goddess: get rich slow

Investing is the most exciting chapter in the life-cycle of a financial goddess. You may get a pleasant surprise out of seeing your savings grow, but you're never going to experience the thrill of watching them soar.

While cash savings are secure rainy day funds, investments are wealth-building tools which, if managed with skill and flair, can make you rich. Of course, if managed poorly, they can end in tears, but that shouldn't happen to you.

To fulfil your true potential as a financial goddess, you have to invest your money in the stockmarket, and to take such an intrepid step, you obviously need to understand a little bit about how financial markets work and behave, and treat them with respect.

Get rich slow

But first, a couple of golden rules. As we said in the first chapter, investing is not about 'doubling your money overnight'. This is not a chapter on 'how to fake it', but is, in the words of the Motley Fool brigade (www.fool.com), an introduction on how to *get rich slow*.

This means building up an investment pyramid layer by layer, from your first £1000 investment, to a five-figure tax-free lump sum. As your portfolio grows in value, and your investing skills improve, you can speculate on higher risk investments which may have phenomenal growth potential long term, like a Chinese fund, or a North American technology fund. But this is not territory for the first (or even second) time investor, who does not have a sufficient foundation of investments to cushion herself against the severe volatility of such markets.

Your first investments must be 'safety-first' ones, progressing in risk profile as the value of your portfolio – and hence the risks it can withstand – grows. And that takes *time*.

Be passionate about investing

Not only does the financial goddess accumulate her wealth over time, indeed over her entire *lifetime*, she is also an 'active' investor.

By active, we don't mean balling out share prices down the phone, and frantically buying and selling stocks every few seconds, like traders on the London Stock Exchange, but taking an active interest in the investments you buy.

Kathryn Langridge, co-head of the Asian funds desk at investment giant Invesco Perpetual, and one the UK's leading managers of Far Eastern funds, says the key to becoming a good fund manager is being 'passionate about money'. Her job is all about picking the right companies to invest in. 'You have to be married to the funds you manage, which means you take them home with you, and the stocks you hold are inside your head all the time,' she says.

Keeping abreast with new changes and developments in your

chosen companies, getting under the skin of what makes the directors tick, measuring them up against the competition, seeking out companies with hidden potential (known as 'under-valued' stocks in City parlance) – this is what investing in the stockmarket is all about.

And it has been proven time and time again, that women who combine thorough company research with hard-headed investment analysis and feminine intuition, regularly beat their male counterparts, who rely on testosterone-fuelled gut instinct to play the investment game.

'In' and 'out' is the mantra for today's stockmarket goddess

The second reason why the twenty-first-century investment goddess must be 'active', is that the stockmarket today is a very different place to what it was in the 1980s and 1990s.

David Schwartz, a stockmarket historian who has spent his career examining stockmarket trends, believes the UK market is likely to remain in a slump for fifteen years, but that there will be several 'sustainable rallies' along the way. 'One of the most important lessons to learn is that "buying and holding" [stocks and shares] is no longer a sound [investment] strategy. It worked well in the final two decades of the twentieth century [when the stockmarket enjoyed a glorious bull run], but the world is different today. The new mantra is "in and out", not "buy and hold".'

Fund manager Anthony Bolton, the darling of London's investment world, has spent three decades working in fund management. He runs his highly successful flagship fund, Fidelity Special Situations, and says he wouldn't usually hold a stock for more than eighteen months.

Your parents and grandparents may have bought a choice few shares, put them away in a drawer, and pocketed a nice profit when they dusted them down several years later, but the 'buy and forget about them' strategy won't work for you any more.

Buy low, sell high

So the ultimate aim of the financial goddess is to 'get in' and 'get out' of the stockmarket (or any other investment: wine, property, art) at the right *time*.

As I'm sure you've heard many times before, this means buying when the price is *low* and selling when it reaches its *high*. Sounds easy. But of course, if playing the stockmarket was really as simple as that, we'd all be billionairesses by now.

While the concept of investing (buy low, sell high) is dead simple, what makes the *art* of investing so darn difficult, is that this is pretty much an impossible thing to accomplish each and every time. So this is where investing skills come into play. As even the world's most eminent stockmarket gurus attest, you simply cannot catch the market wave each and every time, so it would be folly to even try.

We can all spot highs and lows in retrospect, and kick ourselves, saying 'that's the price we *should* have sold at', or 'they're the stocks or funds we *should* have bought'. Like so many other things, investing in hindsight is easy; investing in the future is not! But there are techniques to master so you can put your money in the stockmarket without throwing caution to the wind.

Take the emotion out of investing

It's often said that investing in the stockmarket is '5 per cent skill and 95 per cent emotion'. If that were true you'd best quit now. Losing all your money on a passionate investment whim will have you sobbing into your FTSE charts, and vowing to leave your money stashed away under the mattress for the rest of your years.

The investment goddess saves herself a great deal of angst and sleepless nights by taking a disciplined approach to investing and *taking the emotion out of the stockmarket game*. How? By setting floors and ceilings.

Financial goddesses do not buy shares or investment funds willy-nilly on impulse. Nor do they follow the herd instinct, like so many of the hapless folk who bought technology stocks in the late nineties. Indeed, the fully-fledged investment goddess is smart enough to realise that when the herd mentality sets in, she's missed that particular boat, and it's time to look elsewhere.

So she does her research, identifies her markets, and takes a disciplined approach to investing by setting herself 'high' and 'low' prices at which she will sell. And she sticks to them, come what may.

Floors and ceilings

There's no point whatsoever in buying a share or investment, without knowing when you're going to sell it. That means setting a *ceiling* price and a *floor* price.

Setting a 'ceiling'

Say, you buy shares in BT at £2, because you believe the company is currently undervalued and has the potential to improve its profits, you might set a *sell price* of £5.50 in the next two years.

Tempting though it is to continue holding them if the price is shooting up and you think it might just hit £7, £8 or even £10 – don't. It's just as likely to come crashing down again to £4, or even £3, and may not recover to the £5.50 level for several years (if ever), which would leave you with much less profit than if you'd sold at your *ceiling* price.

When you did your research (be it news analysis, technical

analysis, whatever) you set your ceiling at £5.50. So when the share hits that price, you *must* sell, and enjoy the profits. If the share does continue rallying to £6.50 or £7, shrug it off, but bear it in mind when setting the ceiling for your next stock. Remember, a wise woman takes modest profits, and *gets rich slow.*

Setting a floor price

But of course, not every share you buy will go up. Despite your thorough research, you might simply have misjudged the share. Even the experts do so from time to time. So as well as setting a 'ceiling price', you also need to set yourself a *floor* price to mitigate the pain of a financial loss.

Again, your research and growing familiarity with the 'psychology' of the stock you have bought will help you decide where to set your floor. But say you set the floor for your £2 BT share at £1.40, and the stock comes crashing down to that level. You *must* swallow your losses and sell immediately. Sure, the share *might* creep up again to £2.10 (or £5.50!), but equally it might plummet to 50p, losing you a hell of a lot more than if you'd sold at £1.40.

Professional traders call the floor price a *stop loss* because it mitigates the amount of money they can physically lose on that share, come what may.

If you buy 100 BT shares at £2, with a 'stop loss' set at £1.40, you know that the **maximum** you can lose on your £200 invest-ment is £60. That's a huge comfort, and makes investing in the stockmarket far less risky than many people think.

Of course, if your hunches prove right, you stand to make a profit of £350! But see how taking a disciplined approach takes the emotion out of investing?

As we say, you won't get it right every time. If you make a small loss, never mind, keep researching, move on and try again. But if you get it right say, eight out of ten times, I'd say you've become a very proficient investment goddess indeed!

Investment funds

So now you understand the basic principles of stockmarket investing, you're probably itching to rush out and buy your copy of the FT, do your research, find a stockbroker, and start trading.

But hold on. You're probably not quite ready to make that leap with individual stocks and shares just yet. Investing in a handful of companies like BT, Boots or Marks & Spencer as your sole stockmarket investments is risky, because if they all crash, you'll lose all your money.

So, to protect yourself against market volatility, and increase your chances of reaping growth, you need to invest in as diverse a *basket* of shares as possible.

The stockmarket is a complicated shopping place, made up of lots of different regional sectors: the UK, Europe, Far East, North America, Latin America, which are all broken up into different themed sectors: technology, leisure, financials, pharmaceuticals, utilities. The trouble is that none of these sectors ever move in tandem: so while the North American technology sector shoots up one month, the UK oil and financial (banks and insurance companies) plummet. While smaller UK companies soar, continental Europe languishes in the doldrums.

Why? Because wars, international crises, consumer sentiment, politics, natural disasters, even the weather, affect market sectors and influence them to move in different ways.

Economists, fund managers, and laymen investors alike are constantly interpreting and analysing market-moving news and events, to gauge which way the markets will move next, but there's no foolproof method of financial stargazing, which is why you need to cast your net as wide as possible.

Timing again!

It's also the very reason why I believe there's no such thing as a fundamentally 'bad' investment sector (as events change, different sectors come around again) but there is such a thing as being in the wrong sector at the wrong *time*.

When a miffed investor says that the technology sector has been an absolute washout, what he really means in nine out of ten instances, is that he failed to go into the sector, and come out of it, *at the right time*. Perhaps in the heady days of the pre-millennium technology bubble, he thought that all Internet stocks were a one-way street to heaven, and didn't bother setting a ceiling or a floor price (very few investors who get carried away with the herd instinct ever do). It's certainly true that there were an awful lot of appalling technology companies (mainly dotcoms) that were never worth the paper they were written on. So if he'd bought those, then yes, he was doomed from the start. But equally, there were many others that would have been very good investments if they had been bought using a disciplined approach (ceiling and floor price) and sold at the *right time*. In the two years to Spring 2000, many technology stocks were rising by 50 per cent a day, then the bubble burst, and in the year to September 2002, the technology sector as a whole fell 44.49 per cent.

Investing in a single sector is risky, so until you've climbed a good way up your investment pyramid, you must invest across a *range* of sectors and shares. This is known as 'not putting all your eggs into one basket'.

But, as we said above, as very few first-time investors have the capital required (at least £10,000) to buy enough different companies across many sectors to create a sufficiently diverse portfolio, they buy a ready-made portfolio, in the form of an 'investment fund'.

A world of variety

The wonderful world of investment funds is as varied as the pralines, toffees and sherbets of a sweet shop.

Investment funds come in several different forms: unit trusts, investment trusts, corporate bonds and, as we saw above, in myriad different 'flavours': UK blue-chip, North American, continental European, Far Eastern, and UK smaller companies.

You can buy funds geared towards producing a regular income – like corporate bond funds, or those aimed solely at producing capital growth. Generally younger investors are advised to go for capital growth funds, and older investors approaching retirement to go for income funds, which pay out monthly dividends, at the expense of capital growth.

However, as we said above, a lot depends on the market climate as well. In the year to September 2002, when the FTSE fell 18 per cent, income-producing funds on the whole performed better than growth funds, while in the latter years of the last century, when the stockmarket was on a roll, anyone who'd bought income funds at the expense of capital growth funds would have been kicking themselves.

The fund manager

Investment funds are created by *fund managers* who pick and choose what stocks to buy, and when to sell them. They usually run their investments against a 'benchmark', which will often be the index in that fund's sector.

So, the fund manager of a UK blue-chip fund will measure his performance against that of the FTSE 100 index. If the FSTE 100 grows by 13 per cent in a year, the fund manager will aim to deliver more than that.

All fund managers *aim* to 'outperform their index', but not all (indeed some would say very few!) succeed, which is why you must choose your funds with care, and manage them *actively*.

Value and growth funds

Fund managers fall into one or two camps: value investors and growth investors.

Value investors buy companies which look cheap at the moment, and sell them off when they reach their true value again.

Growth investors put their money into talent. They scour the market for little-known companies that they believe will be tomorrow's success stories and hold them until their potential has translated into profits. This is what technology investors did in the late 1990s.

What is ironic is that yesterday's growth stocks have become today's value stocks, and vice versa. Growth funds fared poorly against value funds in 2002, but market moods change, and investors need to move along with them.

Picking your investments

So how do you pick a good investment? Just as keen followers of fashion keep an eye on seasonal changes on the catwalks, investment goddesses read the financial pages of newspapers to keep abreast with economic moods and company news.

They also keep an eye on investment fund tables found at the back of specialist monthly money magazines like *Moneywise* or the *Financial Mail on Sunday's Money*. These glossies not only record the performance of investment funds in different sectors over one, three and five years, usually at the back of the magazine, but also report on fund managers.

When scouring the tables, you'll obviously be drawn to funds that have delivered a consistently good performance over several years. But as the small print always says, past performance is no guarantee of future returns, so you must look beyond just the annual growth figures.

The key to picking a good investment is to:

a) select the right sector or type of fund for the *time* (UK equity growth, income, European growth, or whatever)
b) pick out funds managed by smart fund managers who really are at the cutting edge of the game. The fund manager is the

linchpin of an investment's success, and everything rides on his or her stock-picking skills.

How are the fund managers doing?

So choosing a good fund manager is crucial. But don't expect it to be easy. In 2002, citywire.co.uk, a financial news website, conducted a groundbreaking investigation into UK investment funds, by scrutinising 863 of the City of London's fund managers. They were unimpressed with more than 700, and awarded only 39 out of the 863 a place in their 'premier league'.

Anthony Bolton of Fidelity, mentioned above, was one of the them. Another was John Dodd, of Artemis, who runs a £180m UK smaller companies fund. In the three years to September 2002, that fund shot up 105 per cent. while the average UK smaller companies fund fell by 23 per cent. Sadly, no women fund managers were awarded a place in the premier league.

Counting the cost: investment fund charges

As well as scrutinising the pedigree of the fund manager, you also need to look at the fund's *charges*.

All investment funds levy charges – supposedly to pay for the skills of the fund manager. These pin-striped men and women are paid handsome salaries and bonuses to look after our money. Sometimes you wonder why.

Funds like unit trusts typically charge between 4 and 5 per cent as an *initial fee*, just for buying the investment; on top of this there will also be an *annual management fee* of 1 to 1.5 per cent, to keep it going. So, if you put £1000 into an investment with a 5 per cent initial charge and a 1 per cent annual management charge, £51 of your money would be swallowed up in charges in the first year, leaving just £949 actually invested.

In addition to initial charges and annual management fees, some investment houses also levy punitive *exit penalties* on their funds, so not only does it cost you to buy the fund, you're also penalised if, having realised it's no good, you want to get your money out again.

Avoid insurance company investments

Endowment policies, which were so oversold in the eighties, have notoriously high charges, to the extent that almost all the investor's first two years' contributions are swallowed in charges.

If you want to sell the policy early (e.g. before the twenty-five years are up) you're penalised with crippling charges again. Women in their forties and fifties who may have been sold an endowment policy in its heyday will be familiar with this. But thankfully, consumer pressure means that the financial services industry has been cleaned up quite considerably in recent years, and twentysomethings are unlikely to be sold this draconian product, and should certainly complain if they are.

We'll be hearing a lot more about endowments in the chapter on mortgages, and also in the last chapter on how to apply for financial compensation. But I brought them up here because many life insurance companies which sell endowments also sell 'investments' which are also loaded with punitive charges. Like premier bank accounts these are something you should avoid. Investments designed by insurance companies are unnecessarily complicated, but given comforting sounding names like 'protected' or 'guaranteed' investments. They promise to deliver at least 5 or 6 per cent growth a year, but will have high charges, and are likely to prove inferior in performance to well-managed unit trust funds from investment houses.

The only true protections against stockmarket volatility are *time* and *active management*. So ignore any investments (from insurance companies or investment houses) which come with any kind of 'promise'.

And, as we said in chapter 3, never buy stockmarket investments from a High Street bank – they simply don't have the expertise to manage investment funds, and their performance is likely to be even worse than those of insurance companies.

Tracker funds and managed funds

The funds we've been discussing so far are known as *managed funds*, because the stocks and shares inside them are picked and *managed* by a fund manager.

But there's another type of stockmarket fund you're likely to come across, and that's the *tracker* fund. While managed funds are looked after by a fund manager, tracker funds are run by computers. The software simply mimics or 'tracks' the movement of a stockmarket index like the FSTE 100 or the Tech Index.

In a bull market, when the index is on an upward curve, there's a very good case for buying a tracker, as your money will grow in tandem with the upward movement of the stockmarket. But this is not such a good bet in a volatile or bear market, as the investment will simply follow the market down again, or mimic its rocky rollercoaster ride.

Indeed, it is in a volatile or bear market that the star fund manager can prove his mettle, picking shares that outwit the generally subdued market mood.

But even the most brilliant fund manager can't get this right every time, so experts usually counsel having an 'index tracker' fund and a 'managed' fund in your portfolio to balance things out.

Because tracker funds are run by computers rather than fund managers, they have much lower charges – typically a 1 per cent initial charge and less than 0.5 per cent annual management charge.

The beauty of regular savings

In the last chapter, we discussed the importance of getting into the habit of making regular monthly savings, or 'paying yourself first'. This should become a life habit for the financial goddess, and one which she brings to investing as well as to saving.

In fact, regular savings are more important in the investment game than ever before, as nothing will offer you better protection against stockmarket volatility than drip-feeding £50 or £100 a month into a 'unit trust fund', as it chortles up and down a rollercoaster ride.

When we were discussing investment funds above, we were talking about *unit trusts*. They are given this name because the funds are made up of several *units*. Each pound you invest in this type of fund buys you a certain number of units.

However, the price of the unit goes up and down with the value of the fund: so when the fund dips in value, the unit price falls and you get more units for your money. Conversely, when the market is high and the unit price rises, you get fewer units for your money.

So, in a volatile market which is constantly going up and down, your regular savings will 'average' out the fluctuations. The technical term for this is *pound-cost averaging*. When drip-feeding money into the stockmarket through regular monthly saving, you don't need to worry too much about getting the timing right because you're constantly ironing out the peaks and troughs of stockmarket volatility anyway.

However, if you just make a big one-off lump sum investment at the wrong time, and the market plummets, you'll have lost a large percentage of your money and may have to wait a very long time for it to climb back up again.

As you can see, I'm a big fan of regular savings into stockmarket funds. It's far less risky than gambling a one-off sum, and as we said in the last chapter it really is *paying yourself*. It's something you can afford to do even while building up a cash reserve. If you have £50 a month to spare, and don't have any investments to your name, I'd strongly urge you to buy a well-managed unit trust, and start reaping the long-term benefits of the stockmarket today.

Keeping it away from the taxman

As we said in the last chapter, you can buy stockmarket ISAs as well as cash ISAs, and these come as mini ISAs, in which you can save up to £3000 a year, and maxi ISAs in which you can save up to £7000 a year.

Many people refer to ISAs as investments but this is confusing. An ISA is just a *tax-free wrapper* like a sweet wrapper, which shields your investments from the taxman. The investment is the unit trust, tracker fund or whatever other type of investment you choose to place inside the ISA wrapper.

Anyone over the age of eighteen, who is resident in Britain for tax purposes, can buy an ISA. The Inland Revenue doesn't give away much, so you'd be mad not to take up the opportunity of allowing your money to roll up tax-free year after year.

Investors traditionally make a beeline for ISAs in the run up to the end of the tax year in early April, but there is no reason why you should wait till then. Tax-free investment planning is a round-the-year exercise, so you should take out an ISA as soon you have the money and have done your research.

Peps

Before ISAs came along in 1999, we had another tax-free savings regime known as PEPs (Personal Equity Plans). Just because PEPs are no longer being sold, this does not mean that you should ignore them if you bought one.

You cannot feed any more money into your PEP investments, but you should keep monitoring them just like your

ISAs, taking profits if you think the funds have reached a peak and moving them elsewhere if they are not performing as well as others in their sector have.

ISAs are a lot more flexible than PEPs when it comes to international companies. Under the PEP regime, you could only hold 25 per cent of your money in foreign stocks, but with ISAs you could put all £7000 of your maxi allowance into a Latin American fund, though I wouldn't recommend it!

Where to buy your investment funds: supermarket sweep

So now you've identified your sectors, swotted up on your fund managers and earmarked £50 or £100 a month to drip-feed into your unit trust. How do you go about buying investments? Go supermarket shopping.

Just as you tend to get a better variety of groceries and more competitive prices at a supermarket rather than at a deli or corner shop, you'll find a wider choice of funds, and benefit from considerably lower charges, at an online funds supermarket.

As we said above, typically an investment house will levy an initial charge of 5 per cent on a unit trust ISA. If you buy from a financial adviser, he or she will keep back 3 per cent of this as commission.

However, when you buy from online fund supermarkets, like Fidelity, Egg, or Chelsea, the initial charge is typically less than 1.5 per cent – sometimes nothing at all. On a £7000 investment this is a saving of £350. Annual management charges are also just a fraction of what they are if you buy direct from the investment house or through a financial adviser.

Like online banks, fund supermarkets allow you to monitor the value of your investments every day, rather than having to wait for statements to be posted to you (usually twice a year). They also have useful research and portfolio management tools to help you pick and choose investments, and keep your investment house in order.

The idea of one-stop fund supermarkets came to Britain from America. One of the largest in the UK is Fidelity Funds network (www.fundsnetwork.co.uk) which offers a choice of 670 different funds; others include Chelsea (www.chelseafs.co.uk), which has 560 funds, and Egg (www.egg.com) which has 263.

Fund supermarkets really are the way forward, they contain so much useful information, and are so simple and efficient to use, that they do away with the need to consult financial advisers, who will be prone to only pushing investments that earn them the most commission.

Building an investment portfolio

The first layer: £1000–£5000 (five years)

Your age, financial aspirations and attitude to stockmarket risk will determine how you go about creating your investment portfolio. As a general rule, the longer you have to invest, the more risk you can afford to take, which is why bullish investors who believe in the long-term potential of markets like China, often invest in such funds to pay for their children's university fees in fifteen or twenty years' time.

But you should not put money into any stockmarket fund unless you can afford to leave it invested there for at least five years. Historically, good stockmarket investments have outperformed returns on cash savings over most five-year periods, but there is no guarantee.

In chapter 2, you wrote your financial CV and defined your financial dreams. You also saw how the typical financial goddess will progress through different financial 'life ages'. This will help you structure your investment portfolio.

If you're a single 28-year-old, have cleared your student debts, bought your first flat, and perhaps have a couple of thousand pounds in cash savings, you're ready to start investing.

Start a regular savings plan

As I said above, the best way to start investing in the stock-market is through regular monthly savings.

Your first investment should be a safety-first one (which usually means investing in your own country), so you may want to start drip-feeding £100 a month into a well-managed UK equity fund, which has delivered good performance over the past three to five years. If it delivers an average return of 8 per cent a year, and you maintain your contributions for five years, you'd have built up £7342 by the time you were thirty-three.

Aim for 8 per cent growth a year tax-free. Good investments will often produce much more than 8 per cent growth a year. Between July 1998 and 1999, Fidelity's managed international fund grew 30.4 per cent. But double digit investment growth year on year is very difficult to achieve, and you'll be building yourself up for disappointment if you go into the stockmarket expecting such results consistently.

Experts agree that you should aim for an aggregate 8 to 9 per cent growth a year tax free – in some years you may get less, others more. That might not sound spectacular thinking back to super stocks that were producing 50 per cent growth a day in the heady days of the technology boom, but it's double the return you'd get from a cash ISA, and your money will really build up over time. Remember your mantra is to *get rich slow*.

Complement your funds

You can only invest in one equity ISA a year, so you want to make sure it's the right one.

You also want to add to that, so you build up a diverse portfolio and increase your chances of reaping growth from as many market sectors as possible over the years.

There's absolutely no point in having two of the same kind of funds (UK, International which covers the same markets) in your portfolio, as you'll simply be duplicating your exposure to certain areas and companies.

Your investment portfolio is really a global jigsaw puzzle of lots of different markets, and you should strive to 'fill in' as many regions and investment sectors as possible over time.

So, if our 28-year-old was given a £1000 lump sum as a birthday present, she might choose to invest that in a UK tracker fund (to balance it against the UK managed fund), or an international fund with holdings in European and North American stocks.

If that performs well, and she finds she has more spare cash as her salary rises, she may well decide to start drip-feeding an extra £50 a month into that fund too, while keeping the UK equity fund she took out two years ago, going.

As we said at the beginning, it's important to be 'active', and keep monitoring the performance of your funds in relation to others in their sector. This will tell you when it is judicious to take profits, or perhaps move your money to another fund.

If markets look as though they may turn gloomy, or you need the money soon (to buy a new car, pay for a wedding or new baby), you may want to transfer some money into cash, so your profits are safe and easy to get to. Managing your investments online will make it much easier to keep track of things, and switch if necessary.

Building your investment portfolio: £5000–£20,000 (five to fifteen years)

If you chose your funds well and maintain your monthly savings, you should, within five years, have built up a very solid foundation layer for your investment pyramid, and become quite familiar with how stockmarket investments work.

Now you want to add more layers. The more investments

you add to your portfolio, the more *active* you have to become in managing them.

An investment portfolio is a bit like a garden: sometimes you need to weed things out, or plant new seeds, and you always need to keep the whole thing pruned and watered for it to blossom and grow.

If you began investing in your late twenties, you will have built up quite a nice nest egg by your early to mid-thirties. You might want to take some of the profits to achieve your financial dreams. Alternatively, you might want to earmark some of your investment portfolio for your retirement fund. We'll be hearing more about this in the pensions chapter.

Add some international flavour to your portfolio

If you have two or three 'safe' investments – e.g. a UK tracker fund, UK equity fund, and a fairly conservative international fund, you should now take a little more risk, perhaps with another international or single sector fund, like a North American fund, property fund, or 'smaller companies' fund, which picks out promising fledgling companies.

By their very nature, these investments are riskier than investing in tried and tested companies, but fund managers have chosen that niche for a reason, which is that they believe there is growth to be unlocked from them.

Your first investment should be a UK fund for the simple reason that it's far easier for a fund manager to keep a watch on companies on home ground than on those abroad. Also, by investing in British funds your money will not be subject to currency fluctuations.

But you'd be holding your portfolio back considerably if you kept all your money in the UK throughout your investment life. So the middle years of your investment pyramid are a good time to go globetrotting.

The Big Apple: the world's largest financial market

Corporate America went through a rough ride in the summer of 2002, but the North American sector as a whole was showing signs of picking up by the end of the year.

We commonly hear the saying: 'When Wall Street sneezes, the rest of the world's markets catch a cold.' It's true, what happens on the American markets really does influence the rest of the world. But no matter how bad things get in the Big Apple, you can't afford to keep your money out of the world's biggest and most influential financial market for ever, so some exposure to American multinationals, either through an international fund, or even a UK fund that holds lots of US companies, is vital.

Reaching for the stars: £25,000–£50,000 (fifteen to twenty-five years)

Forty and fiftysomething couples who have been using their annual ISA allowance of £7000 each into a maxi ISA or £3000 into mini cash and equity ISAs, will have built up quite a fat investment portfolio, and climbed a good way up the investment pyramid.

Through dabbling in several different markets, they will have become proficient stockmarket investors, and may wish to speculate a spare £1000 on a risky fund like a technology or Chinese fund.

As they come closer to retirement, they will also want to start moving some of their money from capital growth to income-producing funds, or cash. As we said above, income-producing funds tend to be regarded as a less risky bet than capital growth ones, because they pay a monthly dividend, which can be useful when you are paying school and university fees, or are retired.

The older you get, the less time you have to invest, so the less risk you should take with your portfolio as a whole, though as we said you may want to earmark a small percentage (say 5 per cent) for high risk, high growth funds, perhaps on behalf of grandchildren.

If you come into an inheritance or large bonus and have used up your annual ISA allowance, you may want to consider investing offshore to protect your money from tax. The pensions chapter will also discuss using part of your ISA investment portfolio as a retirement fund.

Having fun with shares – investment clubs

Although it's best to start investing through readymade funds, many women relish the idea of buying shares of their own. And as we've seen, research proves they can be very good at it!

Picking shares can be fun and, provided you set yourself 'floors' and 'ceilings', not too risky either. Unlike buying an investment fund, when buying your own shares you are in control of the companies you invest in. And although stock-brokers levy dealing costs, you will not have to pay any initial charges or annual management costs to a fund manager.

Setting up an investment club

One of the best ways of investing in shares as a beginner (or even an experienced investor), is through an investment club.

Investment clubs comprise five or more members who each put a small amount (say £25 a month) into the club's kitty. The club then collectively invests in the companies it chooses. This is a lot less frightening than buying shares yourself, as you all knock your heads together to decide what to buy and sell. As you're pooling funds, it's a lot cheaper too.

There are hundreds of investment clubs around the country. Most meet on a monthly basis to review their portfolio, air their research, and decide if they should sell any of their stock or buy new companies.

Perhaps you have a group of friends at work or at your gym who would be interested in forming an investment club. In the UK, Proshare, a non-profit making body, looks after the administration of investment clubs. It produces a helpful manual which explains how to set up a club, elect a secretary and treasurer, and what to do when a member wants to leave the club and take their profits. If you're thinking of setting up a club, obtain a copy of the manual, and go from there.

Alternative investments: wine

The stockmarket isn't the only place to invest. Many people buy wine as an investment and do very well out of it.

The best thing about investing in wine is that if it doesn't reap profits you can always drink it! In fact experienced wine investors buy a handful of cases with the very aim of leaving one behind to drink!

Buy the best wines you can afford

A few golden rules: you must buy from a reputable broker like Berry Bros & Rudd, John Armit, or Farr Vinters in the UK. You should also buy the best quality wines you can afford: Bordeaux wines are classified into five ranks, and perceived to be the 'blue chips' of the market.

Basically, you want to buy wine young and sell when it matures, and the better the wine is, the longer it will take to mature (sometimes fifteen or twenty years). Port can be good as a very long-term investment, but never buy champagne as an investment, there is no market for it.

Your wine broker will be your mentor, so it's important to form a good relationship with him or her. He or she will also take commission when you sell. You should also store your wines 'in bond' in a warehouse to avoid paying VAT on them.

Costs and returns

Storage costs about £6 per case, per year; you will also have to pay to release the wines to drink, so factor all this into the costs. You can pick up a reasonable case of twelve bottles for £300, and add to your cellar from there.

Gary Boom, co-founder of the wine broking and investment company Bordeaux Index, who used to work in the City, reckons wine is one of the safest investments around, and that for the past thirty years, they have consistently outperformed the FTSE 100!

Others are less sanguine, but a couple of cases of fine vintage will certainly add glamour to your investment portfolio, and as we said, if it doesn't turn out to be a bankable commodity you can always drink it.

6

A goddess' home is her palace: property and mortgages

There's nothing like a housing boom to bring out the worst in the British! Property prices are frequently the number one topic of conversation at dinner parties, and fill acres of column inches in newspapers. With house prices having outstripped wage inflation by a terrific margin in recent years, and in certain 'hotspots' even doubled in less than two years, many home-owners can gleefully say that their house is currently earning more than they are.

Homeownership is certainly an essential financial vitamin for the financial goddess. But you have to go about it sensibly – remember the property crash of the late eighties? Just like stocks and shares, property prices can go down as well as up.

A mortgage is the biggest financial commitment you're ever likely to take on. The canny financial goddess spends time scouring the mortgage jungle for the best deals, before she even starts looking for property. She scrutinises carefully the penalties and restrictions of initial low-cost rates, rather than making a beeline for the cheapest rate going.

She is careful not to overstretch herself; in fact, she even considers putting some of her savings towards her mortgage, to save herself thousands of pounds in interest over the years. She maintains her property well, and insures the building and her contents with the best value insurance she can find. She is also mindful of the fact that her home is one of the most expensive purchases she may ever make, and unlike many other consumer goods, not one she can take back if she makes a mistake!

Property as an investment

A goddess' home is her palace, but property can be more than just a roof over your head. Investment property is becoming an increasingly common alternative to pensions as a retirement planning tool.

Because property is a tangible investment, many investors prefer it to stocks and shares. By using equity from your main property to put down a deposit on an investment property, you can build up a very lucrative property portfolio.

Students with parents able to stump up a deposit and act as mortgage guarantors can buy a home in their university town, pay the mortgage by renting out spare rooms, and get a head start on the property ladder. And cheap air travel and competitive mortgages for overseas' property, have made that dream second home in France or Spain more accessible than ever before.

The first-time buyer

In November 2002, the average national house price in Britain was £130,000. In London, it was £249,000. But there were plenty of frustrated house hunters having difficulty finding properties even at those prices: a two-bedroom flat in west London with enough room to swing a cat and kitchen big enough to actually cook in, could have easily set you back £350,000, and more than double that in Mayfair.

If you're an animated first-time buyer, forget the fantasy lifestyle purveyed in hip sitcoms like *Friends* and *Frasier*. It's hard enough to secure a small two-up, two-down as a high-flying professional couple, let alone afford a rambling loft apartment share in a mansion block in the centre of town as a waitress.

Look for up and coming areas

Fashionable postcodes in the major cities may be out of your reach. But cities and towns are constantly being regenerated, and such fringe areas are always a good bet for the first-time buyer.

You can spot up and coming areas by looking out for smart coffee shops opening up, tube extensions or international rail links being built, and new shopping centres being developed. One first-time buyer said: 'When looking for a flat in London, I picked out all the postcodes with the highest crime rates!' While that has probably added a few pounds to her home insurance, it's certainly ensured that she got onto the ladder, and the value of the property has gone up considerably.

Leaseholds

If you're buying a flat, you're likely to be buying a 'leasehold' property which means that although you own the building, you will have to pay ground rent and service charges to the 'freeholder'.

Leases on flats range from ten to 999 years, and when the lease expires you no longer own the property, so it's important not to buy a property with a short lease (less than ninety-five years).

You can apply to extend the lease once you have been in the property for two years, but it can be expensive and will require legal advice. Most mortgage lenders will not advance a loan on flats with a lease of less than eighty years, as such flats are difficult to sell.

Service charges

You should also factor in the cost of ground rent and service charges. A flat in a plush mansion block with lifts and a concierge, or a spanking new development with underground parking and on-site gym, will have much higher service charges than an ex-council block with a concrete staircase!

Don't give up

Spiralling prices, student debts and a general shortage of housing have made purchasing that elusive first home more of a challenge for today's crop of financial goddesses than for their parents.

But don't give up. It's not impossible, you may just need to take a more creative approach than previous generations did. This could mean taking a helping hand from your parents, pooling resources and buying with friends, or taking advantage of the government shared ownership scheme, or other incentives for 'key workers' like teachers and nurses.

A hand up from your parents

Sociologists believe we're entering an age of 'lifetime parenting' in Britain today.

In France and Italy, it's common for young people to live with their parents until they set up home with a permanent partner. In traditional British-Asian families it's the norm for new brides to live with their parents-in-law throughout their married life. But the typical pattern for young Brits is to flee the parental nest in their late teens when they go off to university or get their first job, share flats with friends in their twenties, then settle down in a place of their own.

However, economic hardship is forcing many young women in their twenties and even thirties to go back to living with their parents temporarily, until they are on a better financial footing. A recent survey found that one in four twentysomethings today lives at home with their parents. An equal percentage of young couples are reported to be delaying marriage until they can afford to buy a place.

Helping out with the deposit

The traditional way of purchasing a home is with a deposit of at least 5 per cent of the property's value, and a mortgage no more than 2.5 times a couple's joint income, or 3.25 times a single buyer's income.

Going by this equation, a single 26-year-old looking to buy a £170,000 flat in London would need an annual salary of at least £49,700, and a cash deposit of £8500, plus an extra £2000 at least for stamp duty, surveys and furniture, which is not a realistic scenario for many.

So youngsters are increasingly turning to their parents for help. In November 2002, the average deposit put down by first-time buyers in London was a whopping £31,100, and mortgage experts say much of this came from parents willing to give or lend money.

But if your parents don't happen to have that kind of capital sitting around, but are still eager to help you out, there are other options available.

Using equity from your parents' home

Many parents who have built up considerable equity in their own homes, release some of this money by increasing their loans or extending the term of their mortgage, to lend money to their offspring.

A couple with a joint income of £50,000 and a £98,500 mortgage on a family home worth £210,000, could borrow an extra £27,000, taking their mortgage to £125,000.

Or, if they don't plan to retire soon, they could extend the term of their mortgage by an extra five or ten years, which would reduce their monthly payments and free up money to help out with their children's mortgage.

If your parents don't like the idea of increasing their own commitments, they can use their savings as 'collateral', by lodging spare cash into an 'offset deposit account', such as that offered by the Woolwich. Their savings would reduce the value of your mortgage so long as it remained in the account.

So, if you needed to borrow £120,000 and your parents could afford to leave £15,000 in the offset account, you would only need to borrow £105,000. Your parents would not earn interest on money kept in this account, but they would retain control of their cash, and could dip into it whenever they needed to (not an option available to you!), though obviously your mortgage would then rise.

100 per cent mortgages and using parents as guarantors

Another strategy becoming increasingly common for young people unable to stump up a deposit, is to take out a 100 per cent mortgage or borrow more than three times their salary, using their parents as 'guarantors'.

By becoming guarantors, your parents agree to make the repayments on your home if you fall into financial dire straits. A lender will usually assess your parents' income and financial commitments to satisfy themselves that they would actually be able to meet these payments if they needed to. Some lenders, like the Newcastle Building Society, will accept grandparents and siblings as guarantors.

Buying with friends

Buying with friends or siblings is also becoming an increasingly popular option. The benefits are that you'll be able to afford a much nicer property, with more space, than if you bought alone.

But you are essentially entering into a business relationship, so it's imperative to take legal advice and draw up contracts, particularly if each of you contributes a different percentage of the deposit.

- As well as working out the equity figures, you should consider the emotional implications of one of you putting down more money, or paying a larger share of the mortgage. Will it affect your relationship as co-habitees?
  Property is not a liquid asset which can be sold at the drop of a hat, so it's vital to discuss things thoroughly first. If the partnership is well planned and discussed it could work out brilliantly but, if not, a tiny misunderstanding could escalate into misery and even financial ruin. Living with friends is not the same as living with a partner.
- Most co-buyers purchase their homes as 'tenants in common', so one party can sell her portion of the home to someone else, who would then become the new co-owner. However, in practice most co-homeowners say it would be easier to just sell up and each take their respective share of the equity. Or if one wants to stay on and could afford it, she could buy the other out.
- You will both be individually and jointly liable for the mortgage, so if one of you defaults on the loan, the other would have to pay up and vice versa.

- As well as the official financial arrangements, sharing of furniture and other household items, bills, decorating, maintenance, and arrangements for entertaining family and friends, should also be discussed.

Due to the complicated nature of buying and sharing a house with other people, it would be unwise to buy with more than two friends, and even then you may find traditional mortgage lenders slightly wary.

Shared ownership

Shared ownership is a government initiative run by housing associations and local councils. It is designed to help people on low wages, who would not otherwise be able to buy, to get onto the housing ladder by buying a proportion of the home (usually anything from 30 to 70 per cent) and paying subsidised rent on the remainder.

After a year, you can increase your stake in the property until you own it fully. If, by the time you come to sell, you own 100 per cent of the home, you would put it on the market in the usual way. If the housing association still retains a share, you would sell the home back to them, but benefit from appreciation of your share.

So, if you bought a 60 per cent share in a £200,000 home and it was worth £300,000 in seven years' time, you would have £180,000 to put towards your next property.

There are over 300 shared ownership schemes around the country, but most have long waiting lists. Applicants are means-tested and may have to pay the housing association's legal costs when increasing their stake in the property or selling.

Most mortgage lenders are happy to advance loans to shared ownership applicants provided they fill the normal criteria. In 1998, rising TV presenter June Sarpong, then just twenty years old, was able to buy a 50 per cent share in a two-bedroom flat in Earls Court under the Notting Hill Housing Association.

The mortgage maze

Choosing a low-cost penalty-free mortgage will save you thousands of pounds over a lifetime, so spend time scouring the market.

Never buy a mortgage from a financial adviser in an estate agency. They will be tied to an insurance firm, and may try to sell you an endowment or, at the very least, home insurance from the company they are tied to.

In our mothers' day, a young couple would save up in a high interest account with their bank for many years, then dress up in their finest clothes to try to impress their bank manager into giving them a mortgage.

Today, there are more than 400 different mortgage deals out there, and banks and building societies will be begging *you* for your custom. Many of the deals aren't even worth considering, and even the best have a catch or two somewhere – as they say, there's no such thing as a free lunch!

Endowment mortgages – avoid them like the plague

The one type of mortgage to shun without a second thought is an endowment mortgage. Endowment mortgages were all the rage in the eighties and early nineties.

They work like this: say you buy a £100,000 flat with an endowment mortgage. You would borrow 90 or 95 per cent of this amount (depending on how much deposit you put down) from a bank or building society, and take out an *endowment policy*, to pay it off.

The endowment should pay off the *capital sum* you borrowed.

However, in return for lending you the princely sum of £95,000 (if you put down a 5 per cent deposit) the bank will, of course, charge you *interest*. So, to pay this off, you will also need to take out an *interest only* mortgage.

What exactly is an endowment?

Endowment policies are complicated stockmarket linked investments, into which you pay monthly premiums. The idea is that at the end of the term you should have built up enough to pay off the *capital sum* you borrowed to buy your home, and have a nice lump sum left over for yourself too.

But the problem is that throughout the eighties and early nineties a large raft of greedy financial salesmen vastly over-projected the rates at which the endowment policies they sold would grow, leaving many poor homeowners with policies that won't even pay off the *capital* borrowed on their homes, let alone provide them with a lump sum. Some homeowners are now facing a shortfall of £10,000. If they don't get compensation, they will need to find this money out of their own pockets, or their mortgages will remain unpaid.

Charges and inflexibility

So why are endowments such bad value? Well, plummeting stockmarkets are partly to blame. But one of the main things that makes endowments such poor investments are the *charges*.

On many endowment policies, you stand to lose your entire contributions for the *first two years* in charges, depriving you of hundreds, if not thousands of pounds.

Endowments are also hideously *inflexible*. If you want to sell the policy before the end of the term, either because you split from your partner, or just want to change to a much safer *capital repayment mortgage*, you'll lose a hell of a lot of money. In fact, if you decide to sell up in the first few years of taking out an endowment, you might even *lose* more money than you've *paid in*.

Sound fair? No. Endowments are inflexible and unreliable, so all new homebuyers should shun them in favour of straight-forward *capital repayment mortgages*, which are *guaranteed* to pay off the loan in the required number of years (provided of course you keep up the repayments!).

What to do if you have an endowment shortfall

Over the past two years, six million people have received letters warning them that their endowments may not pay off their mortgage.

The letters are coloured like traffic lights: a red one indicates that you're likely to have a serious shortfall, an amber one that you might experience a shortfall, a green one means you might just be okay. If you've received a red- or amber-coloured letter, you have one of three options:

- Auction your policy. If your endowment policy is a *with-profits* one, and has been running for more than seven years, you can *auction* the policy, often for a small profit. There are a couple of firms which specialise in this, one of them is Beale Dobie. It compiles a list of life insurers whose policies it will accept, and will give a no-obligation quote on application.
- Remortgage onto a capital repayment mortgage. However, if you have a *unit-linked* policy, it cannot be auctioned. Contact your life insurer to establish exactly how much the shortfall will be. Then consider: Either stopping the policy, and putting the money you get from your endowment into a straightforward *capital repayment* mortgage. This way you'll know for sure that you will pay off the loan in a certain number of years. Or, if you can afford to keep paying into the endowment and making the repayments on a new

repayment mortgage, you may decide to keep the endowment going as an 'investment'. You'll need to do a fair bit of number-crunching, and weighing up of pros and cons, to decide what strategy is best for you.

- Make additional savings into an ISA. Another way to make up the shortfall is to start making additional savings into a cash or stockmarket-based ISA. If you choose a good stockmarket-based ISA, it should outperform your endowment, and if you have more than five years left to pay off your mortgage, this might be worth considering.

Some insurers suggest increasing your premiums to help the endowment reach its target sum. I have to say, if someone suggested to me that I should put more money into a policy which had already underperformed significantly, I'd be reeling.

Apply for compensation

The last chapter gives a step-by-step guide to applying for compensation if you think you may have been missold an endowment.

In November 2002, the *Mail on Sunday* conducted its own 'name and shame' list of insurers which had sold appalling endowments in the products' heyday. It branded: Alba Life, Guardian, Eagle Star, Friends Provident, Scottish Widows and Royal & Sun Alliance among the worst culprits.

The Financial Services Authority has agreed to compensate victims of Abbey Life, which sold some shockingly bad policies in the eighties. However, if you have a policy from one of the above named insurers, and you have been informed that it is likely to produce a shortfall, it's certainly worth lodging a complaint.

Repayment mortgages: a choice of rates

So what exactly is a *capital repayment* mortgage? In simple terms, it's a very large loan that you take out to buy a house, and repay over several years (the usual term is twenty-five years), at a fairly competitive rate of interest.

If you take out a typical bank loan, you will usually be charged interest at several percentage points above the Bank of England's base rate (indeed often double or triple that figure). However, many mortgage rates are *fixed* at an interest rate considerably lower than the base rate, or *discounted* by a couple of percentage points from the lender's variable rate (usually a bit higher than the Bank of England's standard rate).

Other fees

But you must look beyond the *headline rate* when evaluating a mortgage deal. In addition to the monthly repayments at the specified rate, there may be a gamut of other fees to pay, which can add a few thousand pounds to the cost of buying the mortgage.

- Nearly all lenders charge a *valuation fee* to assess whether (in their opinion) your prospective home is worth the money they are lending. This can cost anything from £150 to £300.
- Some will also charge an *arrangement fee* for making the money available to you; this can cost up to £350.
- On top of this, if you are borrowing more than 80 per cent of the value of the home, many lenders will also charge your for an *mortgage indemnity guarantee* (MIG). Basically, this is insurance that covers *them* against you defaulting on the loan, except that they want *you* to pay for it! MIGs can add a couple of thousand pounds to the cost of your mortgage so this really is something to try to avoid.

Redemption penalties

However, in addition to MIGs and valuation fees, the other sting in the tail of many mortgages is *redemption penalties*.

This is basically a penalty you will have to pay if you want to move house, pay off a chunk of your mortgage early, or simply move to a better rate. Redemption penalties usually work out at *three months' interest*, so it can be jolly expensive to walk away from such a tie-in.

Lenders use redemption penalties to 'lock' customers into staying with them. They are often levied on temptingly low *fixed rates* over one-, two- or five-year periods, so they give with one hand, and take with the other. So, say a lender is sporting a fantastically low rate of 1.99 per cent for one year. When that honeymoon period comes to an end, you're more than likely to revert to paying the bank's standard variable rate (which can be as much as 5.99 per cent) and be locked into this for up to five years. If you want to move, you'll have to pay the redemption penalty.

As a general rule, the lower the fixed rate, the more likely it is that the lender will levy redemption penalties, which is why it's so important to look at the *deal as a whole* rather than just the headline offer.

Discounted, capped and tracker rates

As well as fixed rates, there are also *discounted* rates, where you pay 1 or 2 per cent below the standard variable rate for a couple of years; *capped* rates in which the bank guarantees that the rate you pay will not exceed the given 'cap'; and *tracker* mortgages, which 'track' the Bank of England's base rate, though often at a slightly higher level.

How to work it out

Many financial websites offer mortgage calculators so you work out your repayments at different rates. Before taking on a mortgage:

- work out the initial rate you would pay if you took a low fixed rate

- then work out the variable rate you would have to pay when the fixed rate comes to an end, plus the redemption penalties you would have to pay if you moved
- add to this valuation fees, arrangement fees and indemnity premiums.

The housebuying process: stamp duty, surveys and insurance

Although rustling up the deposit is usually the biggest hurdle to buying your first home, it isn't the only expense you'll have to dig deep into your pockets for. There's also stamp duty, legal costs, surveys, insurance, and moving costs, which put together, can easily add an extra £3000 to the bill.

Putting in an offer – start low!

When you have found your ideal home, you need to put in an offer. No doubt you'll hear stories of hoards of eager buyers chasing far too few properties. But don't be afraid to start bidding low (£5000–£10,000 below the asking price), particularly if you can afford to let one or two places slip out of your hands. You never know the full story behind a property which comes onto the market, and it'll give you good experience of what can go on.

I made an opportunistic offer of £15,000 less than the asking price on my home, and eventually got it for £12,500 less. What I didn't know at the time of making the offer was that the vendors had just lost a buyer, who had put in an offer some six months previously. He had held out for several months while the vendors looked for a property for themselves, but eventually lost patience. As fate would have it, the vendors then found somewhere just as their first buyer pulled out. It was around this time that I viewed the property. I liked the interior but wasn't keen on the fact that the property needed a new roof and windows, so I put in a low offer, and 'forgot' about it. Three weeks later, the estate agent called to say he thought we could do a deal. The vendors had finally found a place they liked, and they didn't want to lose another buyer, so a slightly lower offer was better than none at all.

As a first-time buyer, with nothing to sell, there was no 'chain' at my end, and the property they wanted to move into was vacant, so it worked well all round. As I say, I had no idea of this, until *after* I'd actually bought the property, but I'd have kicked myself if I'd paid any more for it! First-time buyers are the feeders of the property chain. If they all dried up, the house chain would collapse, so bear this in mind when you put in your offer.

Surveys

Once your offer has been accepted, you'll need to get a *survey* done.

The survey is really a healthcheck to ensure that the roof and brickwork are in good condition, and that there are no severe problems with damp, subsidence or wiring. Surveys can cost anything from £250 to £500.

If your surveyor comes back with scores of points which will cost many thousands of pounds to put right, you may want to renegotiate your offer to reflect the costs, or indeed pull out of the sale altogether.

Many experts believe it's unfair for buyers to have to stump up the cost of the survey, and moves are in place to introduce 'sellers' packs' so the vendor would supply these details and the buyer would know exactly what state the property was in when they bought it. This would certainly help speed up the property buying process.

Conveyancing and local authority searches

You will also need to appoint a solicitor to administer the sale. This is known as *conveyancing*, and can cost anything from £350 upwards.

Your solicitor will also undertake a *local authority search* to ensure the council isn't planning to erect a petrol station in your back garden. This will cost about £150. On top of this, there will also be a £100 *land registry fee*.

Stamp duty

But by far the biggest single expense of buying a home, apart from the deposit, is the *stamp duty*.

The Inland Revenue levies 1 per cent stamp duty on purchases between £61,000 and £250,000, 3 per cent duty on purchases up to £500,000 and 4 per cent on properties over that, adding an immediate £2,000 to the cost of a £200,000 flat. Stamp duty usually has to be paid within a month of moving in.

Exchanging contracts

Once you have completed your surveys and decided to buy, you will *exchange contracts* with your vendor. This usually happens two weeks before moving in. This is also the date on which you will pay your deposit.

If you pull out of the sale after exchanging contracts you will lose your deposit, and may also have to reimburse your vendor's costs, so make sure you are absolutely sure you want to go ahead, before signing on the dotted line.

Moving in!

The day of the move, your mortgage lender will electronically transfer the amount you have borrowed to buy your home to your solicitor, who will in turn pass it onto your vendor's solicitor. When this transaction has gone through, the sale has been completed, you can drive down to the estate agent, collect your keys, and move in!

Girls' guide to home maintenance

Cowboy workmen and leery builders are the bane of career girls and single mothers. But the good news is that female plumbers, decorators and builders are slowly creeping into the business, adding a woman's touch to all those jobs that need doing around the house. Apart from the obvious security benefits, the Ms Fixits of this world tend to be more respectful of their clients' homes, and pay better attention to detail than their male colleagues.

Women and Manual Trades (WAMT), which was established in 1975 to encourage women to join non-traditional manual trades, publishes a directory of tradeswomen. It's a good idea to keep a copy in your financial housekeeping file. And, if you fancy taking up the tools yourself, women's education in building (WEB) runs courses in carpentry, joinery, plumbing and electrics.

Dripping taps or burst pipes from a cold spell can cause havoc in your property. Furiously flicking through the *Yellow Pages* in such a moment of crisis is guaranteed to be a disaster. So ask around and, *before* you actually have a problem, build up a list of reliable plumbers, electricians, locksmiths and drain experts you can call.

Adding value to your home

Certain home improvements will add more value to your property than others. Top of your list should be: a well-maintained roof, double-glazed windows with security locks, up-to-date electrics and damp proofing.

Gas central heating will cost about £3000 to be installed professionally, but you'll recoup 80 per cent of the costs. And while estate agents may wax lyrical about state-of-the-art kitchens and bathrooms, experts say you should spend no more than 10 per cent of the value of your home on a new kitchen. You should spend no more than 7 per cent on a new bathroom, though you would recoup 60 per cent of the cost of installing a good shower.

If you are putting your property on the market, give it a good facelift. Give all those fences and doors a good lick of paint, replace the mouldy shower curtain, arrange your furniture stylishly, and make use of mirrors and lighting to present your home in the best possible light.

Moving up the property ladder

If buying a property as a first-time buyer was expensive, selling your home and moving up the ladder is even more so. This time round, you'll have to pay estate agents' fees to sell (unless you do it yourself), on top of all the other costs involved with buying.

Babies and young families

Most young couples find they need to move home when their first baby comes along. Babies may be tiny but they eat space, and things which didn't bother you as a carefree couple, like a tight doorway which won't accommodate a pushchair, bathrooms on different levels to the bedrooms, or lack of parking space outside your front door, could turn out to be a real pain.

High flying couples who have built equity in property individually may be able to afford their ideal family home by selling up two flats, so their mortgage repayments will remain more or less the same. But it would be unwise to increase your mortgage too drastically, particularly if you are planning to stop work for a few years or save for school fees.

Many young families find that the 3 per cent stamp duty on property between £250,000 and £500,000 really bites. Rising prices mean that many couples with growing families are releasing equity from their home to stay put and build loft conversions to accommodate their growing family, rather than enduring the costs and traumas of moving.

Investing in property

Taking out a second mortgage on an investment property with a view to letting the flat or house out, known as 'buy-to-let', has become increasingly popular in recent years.

The idea is that the rental income will cover the mortgage, insurance and maintenance costs, and also leave you with a little profit, while the property itself will also have risen in value by the time you come to sell. Buy-to-let investors generally choose one- or two-bedroom flats in university towns, or in cities with multinational companies with a large mobile workforce.

The tax trap

However, although property has proven to be a great investment in recent years, there are traps to be wary off. The main thing is *capital gains tax*.

All property, other than your main residence, is subject to *capital gains tax* at 40 per cent when you come to sell. So, if you buy a flat for £100,000 and sell it for £200,000 six years later, you may have to hand over up to £40,000 of that profit to the Inland Revenue (we all have a *capital gains tax allowance* which was £7700 in 2002 to 2003. So if this was your only profit that was subject to CGT the bill would be £32,300).

Void periods, letting agents and insurance

On top of this, you also have to factor in for void periods, when you do not have tenants but still have to make the mortgage repayments.

You will have to insure and maintain the property and, if you enlist a lettings agent to find tenants and look after the day-to-day running, they can take up to 15 per cent of the rental income as commission.

Mortgages and creating a portfolio

There are several specialist lenders offering buy-to-let mortgages, though most will require at least a 20 per cent deposit and will also charge a slightly higher rate than normal mortgages.

Experienced investors build up a property portfolio by snapping up rundown places, sprucing them up, selling them off for a quick profit and using this capital to put down a deposit on one or two other flats which they can let out, gain a rental income from and build up capital appreciation.

Investing in property as a student

Parents have been buying up terraced houses and flats for their children studying away at university for years. However, it has become particularly popular in recent years, as prices in the popular cities of learning like Oxford, Manchester, Edinburgh and Leeds have soared.

But not all university towns are a good bet. Provincial cities like Hull already have a surplus of cheap houses, and property prices around the university area actually fell by 15 per cent in 2001.

How to do it

- Buy property close to the campus. In general, it's also best to buy a smaller property (no more than four bedrooms), as these are less likely to get trashed at wild student parties. Buying in a touristy town will also offer opportunities for letting out the property in the summer vacations when students have left.

- Make the purchase in your own name, with your parents acting as guarantor for the mortgage. If the property is bought in your parents' name and it is not their main residence, they'll be liable to pay capital gains tax on the sale.

- Any renovation undertaken after tenants have moved in, can be offset against the rental income for tax purposes. However, your parents should ensure that they can maintain the mortgage payments over the holidays, perhaps by requiring tenants who wish to keep the room for the next term to pay a retainer.

Buying a home abroad

Low interest rates, cheap travel and better weather are luring rising numbers of Brits to buy that dream second home abroad.

Property in France, Spain and Italy is undoubtedly better value than in Britain. For £150,000 you could buy a rustic four-bedroom stone house in Brittany, a two-bedroom apartment in the sixteenth arrondissement of Paris, or even something in the Dordogne.

If renovating, maintaining and renting out a farmhouse in the depths of the French countryside isn't your thing, you can snap up a chic two-bedroom flat with a view of the sea and a rooftop swimming pool on the glamorous Côte d'Azur for less than £200,000. Such places are easy to lock up and leave, and to rent out in high season.

New properties in France have a two-year guarantee on fixtures and fittings and a ten-year building guarantee. Buying costs, legal fees and stamp duty are also much lower than on properties which are more than seven years old.

Avoid euro mortgages

Although euro interest rates are currently lower than British, it is safer to take out a mortgage in sterling, as currency fluctuations could push up your repayments.

The market for overseas mortgages in Britain is growing, and many brokers offer competitive rates. The maximum loan value on most continental properties is 75 per cent, and the maximum term is usually fifteen years on a French property.

It is vital to take legal advice from a specialist familiar with the country you are buying in. You will also have to pay capital gains tax when selling an overseas property, though this can be avoided by buying through an offshore company.

7

Pensions:
aging abundantly

Most women spend a disproportionate amount of their lives worrying about getting older, to no avail. Research suggests that older people are actually happier people!

But a growing aging population is also presenting today's befuddled government with one of the biggest challenges of modern times: what are they, and future generations, going to live off?

Britain's pensions timebomb

By 2025, the number of over-fifties in Britain will have risen by more than six million, but the number of under-fifties will have fallen by one and a half million. So, by the time today's teenagers reach the age of eighty, half the British population could consist of pensioners!

Not only will there be more pensioners around, they're also going to be spending a lot longer in retirement.

At the moment, the state retirement age for women is sixty

(for men sixty-five). But higher living standards and better health care mean many of today's young women could live fighting fit to the age of eighty or eighty-five. That means we could spend a quarter of a century or more in retirement. And some of us could even end up spending more years in retirement than in work!

Fine if we're assiduously making financial provisions to pay for it. But the problem is we're not, by a long shot. As newspapers expose on an almost daily basis, we're grossly underestimating the cost of this extended holiday, and woefully underfunding our pension plans.

Pensions might sound boring, but poverty in old age is hardly a barrel of laughs either.

Poverty in old age

If you think the day when you'll be reaching for your bus pass and reading glasses is a long way off, and that somehow 'things will miraculously take care of themselves', fast forward your life twenty, thirty-five or forty years from now.

Picture yourself shivering in a freezing flat worrying about heating bills when you're too old and frail to run around. Imagine having to scrimp and save for every penny when you do your grocery shopping. Picture not being able to afford emergency health care, or a new pair of glasses. And imagine enduring twenty or twenty-five years of this grim existence. That's the true of cost of ignoring pension planning.

How big is the problem?

So just how big is the pension shortfall? Well, JP Morgan Fleming, an investment house, believes that more than half of Britain's current working population is likely to retire on an income of less than 40 per cent of their current salary. And government research shows there's a whacking £27 bn gap in the amount we will need to live off comfortably in retirement, and the amount we're actually saving each year.

Volatile stockmarkets, poor-value personal pensions, insurance company debacles like Equitable Life, and employers shutting down final-salary pension schemes at the rate of knots, have created a chilling pensions crisis in Britain today. But unless we start addressing this problem now, by planning to retire *later* and save *more*, we're storing up for ourselves a bleak and vulnerable few decades in our twilight years.

The financial goddess has no intention of getting left out in the cold. She has a pensions strategy which forms the backbone of her financial lifeplan. And she keeps it under constant review, as she moves through every life age, to ensure she's on track to build up a fund fat enough to pay for all those painting holidays and cruises round the Med, books she never had time to read when she was so busy working, and maybe even a savings plan or two for her grandchildren!

Pension planning

The earlier you start the better

Retirement's a long way off. Why start fretting now? Because: a) Your retirement fund is the largest investment you'll make in your lifetime. By the time you come to retire, your 'pension' should be worth a lot more than your home – that should give you an idea of what a terrifyingly expensive business it is. b) As we explained in the investment chapter, the longer you leave your money invested, the more chance it has to grow and grow. So the sooner you get cracking the better.

Never too late to start

But it's *never* too late to start! If you've ignored making pension provisions for yourself through your twenties, thirties and early forties, either because you left it all to your husband, or simply through apathy, ignorance or fear, ten or fifteen years of hard savings now could still make a vast difference to your standard of living when you retire. Even if you're in your early fifties and have no pension to your name, it's better to start saving now, than suffer later.

But, as we've said, pensions aren't the only way of building up a retirement fund. Indeed, a growing army of investors are losing faith in the system. This chapter explains how the current state pension system works, and guides you through the maze of company and personal pensions, ISAs and property to help you devise a retirement fund strategy. There's no right or wrong way. What is crucial is that you ensure that you are saving *enough* to retire abundantly.

How much is 'enough'?

So just how big a pension will you need – £500,000, £1m, £2m, £10m? It might sound crass to ask a 25-year-old when she'd like to retire, but that does form the basis of pension planning.

In order to work out how much you need to start saving, you need to know:

a) how many years you've got to save
b) how much you'll need to live off when you stop working.

Aim to build a fund that will pay *two-thirds* of your final working salary. Unless you plan on living like a hermit and stashing away every last penny throughout your working life, it's unrealistic to expect to retire on a pension equivalent to 100 per cent of your final salary.

The 'model' pension is one equal to two-thirds of your final salary. So, if your final salary was £25,000, you should aim to have built up a 'pension' worth £16,500 a year by the time you retire. If you've paid off the mortgage, and have other savings and investments put by, this should be enough to enjoy a reasonably comfortable life in your golden years.

Part of the reason why the pension system in Britain is in such a crisis, is that it was modelled on a society that would dutifully save from the ages of twenty-one to sixty, and spend just five to ten years in retirement. However, as we saw above, that equation doesn't work anymore. There are plenty of 28-year-olds around who still haven't settled into permanent employment, and lots of robust sixty-somethings who are far from ready to hang up their boots!

What is a pension anyway?

So what exactly is a pension? How does it work? How does it grow? How will it provide an income in your golden years?

Many women fall into that common trap of believing that just because they have got a 'pension' of some sort, they're automatically sorted on the retirement-planning front, even if they haven't put a penny into the fund for years, and it's actually only worth a few hundred quid!

Pensions aren't magic. They're simply very large funds, accumulated over a lifetime, that will provide you with an income when you stop earning (provided of course that you save enough into them!).

But pensions also come with all sorts of catches (and a few benefits), which you have to be fully aware of before committing your money.

If you're a younger investor, you should also be mindful of the fact that a future government may change the pension regime at any time. Another reason why it's so important to keep your strategy under constant review!

How do pensions work?

Tax relief

The overwhelming benefit of saving into a pension is that the government gives you tax relief on your contributions. This is really money for free.

If a basic-rate taxpayer puts £778 of her own money into a pension, the Inland Revenue will make that up to £1,000. A higher-rate taxpayer need only save £600 to get £1,000, as tax relief is offered at the higher rate too.

So, putting your money into a pension guarantees you an automatic profit on day one, which is a rather nice inducement. However, there are numerous downsides too:

- You have to leave your money invested until you are at least fifty.
- You can then take 25 per cent of the fund you have built up as a tax-free lump sum. So if your fund was worth £100,000, you could get your hands on £25,000 tax free.
- But you are obliged to buy an *annuity* with the remaining 75 per cent.

What is an annuity?

An *annuity* guarantees you an annual income for the rest of your life. When you come to retire, you must trade in your pension fund for an annuity from a life insurance company. Regardless of whether you live for another five or fifty years, your annuity provider *guarantees* that you will receive an income for the rest of your years.

That's the comfort of having an annuity. However, the cruel downside is that if you die prematurely, your annuity company simply pockets the money. Pensions cannot be passed down to your heirs (though company pensions do include a widow/er's pension). So, if a woman who had been saving into a pension since the age of thirty retired and bought her annuity at sixty, then passed away at the age of sixty-two, she'd have drawn the short straw.

Indeed, it's the unfairness of the annuity system – the fact that you don't really own your pension – that deters so many savers from it.

The pension system is under constant review. Many experts believe there is a good chance that the annuity system will have been overhauled by the time today's crop of twenty- and thirty-something financial goddesses retire. But for the time being that's the situation and, if you are saving into a pension, you have to be aware of it.

The state pension system

We pay taxes and National Insurance for lots of reasons. One of them is so that the government will help to support us in our old age.

But as we said, the shifting demographics of an aging population and diminishing workforce mean the future of the state pension is uncertain to say the least.

The state currently provides a basic pension to citizens who have made sufficient National Insurance contributions. Any woman who has paid NI contributions for at least 90 per cent of her working life (which equals approximately thirty-nine years) could, in 2002, claim the basic pension of £75.50 a week from the age of sixty.

Married women who have not built up NI contributions through paid work, are entitled to a married woman's pension of £45.20 a week, based on their husband's NI contributions. But they can only claim this once their husband starts drawing his pension at the state retirement age of sixty-five.

Married women's pension scandal

However, a major pensions scandal was unearthed in 2002 when it came to light that 4.5m married women in Britain who had opted to pay a 'reduced rate' of NI contributions known as the 'married woman's stamp' had in fact built up little or no pension entitlement of their own.

The married woman's stamp was introduced after the Second World War, and women who opted for it paid just a third of the full NI contribution rate. In return for this reduced rate, they gave away any entitlement to contributory state benefits, including the state pension and unemployment benefit. But you'd have expected them to get something.

Researchers at the independent House of Commons library calculated that these women had paid a total of £8.2bn in reduced rate NI contributions since the mid-1970s, but are now getting absolutely nothing for it. It has led to many MPs dubbing the 'married women's stamp' the 'biggest pensions scandal ever'.

Boosting your state pension

Clearly you won't be able to live like a queen on the basic state pension, but there are many ways you can boost your state pension.

In April 2002, the government launched a state second pension, which is basically a 'top up' pension linked to earnings (though anyone earning less than £10,000 a year at 2001/2002 would be treated as though they were actually earning £10,000).

You may also be entitled to a second state pension if you cannot work through long-term illness or disability, if you are needed at home, or have low earnings because you are caring for a disabled person or child under the age of six.

State second pension

The state second pension replaced the state earnings-related pension scheme (SERPS), which, as the name suggests, is an earnings-related pension.

Basically, through SERPS, higher earners who had been in employment since 1978 built up a larger state pension than those on lower earnings. Employees were automatically included in SERPS unless they or their employers opted for them to be 'contracted out'.

Those who 'contracted out' of SERPS gave up their entitlement to this higher state pension, and built up a replacement in their company's occupational scheme or a personal pension instead. In return for giving up this additional benefit, they either paid less money in NI contributions, or had a part of their NI contributions rebated into a personal pension.

The government has indicated that it plans to make the state second pension a flat rate rather than an earnings-linked pension in a few years' time. But it must be remembered that future governments can change state pensions at any time, so it is unwise to rely on schemes currently in place being available when you come to retire.

Private pensions

Of course financial goddesses have no intention of relying on the state pension. There are many routes to building up that seven-figure retirement fund, and these are outlined below.

Company pensions

If your employer offers a company pension scheme, you'd be well advised to join it. Not only do employers have to contribute to their company pension schemes, they also have to make annual increases so the contributions keep up with inflation.

Many company pension schemes also come with a range of other benefits, which, as we saw in chapter 3, would be expensive to purchase yourself.

These may include:

- life insurance which pays a lump sum to your dependants if you die within service
- a pension if you have to retire early due to ill health
- pensions for your widow(er) when you die.

Employers must give new employees information about their company pension within two months of joining even though they may not be eligible to join the scheme immediately.

If you have not joined your company scheme because you don't understand it, contact the personnel department, as you are effectively turning down a pay rise. There will be some paperwork, but it should be straightforward enough, and provided you remain with your employer for at least two years, you can transfer the pension benefits you build up.

Final-salary pensions

One of the best company pension schemes around is the final-salary pension, which pays a percentage of your final salary on retirement depending on the number of years you have worked with the company.

The typical model is to accrue a pension of one-sixtieth of your salary for each year worked. So, if you worked for your firm for ten years on a salary of £24,000, you would be guaranteed to get a pension of £4000 a year.

The beauty of final-salary pensions is that your employer shoulders the risks of ensuring that there is enough money in the pension pot to pay your pension, and as it is based on length of service and salary it is relatively easy to forecast how much you will get.

However, in a volatile market this works out expensive for employers, so many of Britain's largest companies have now closed their final-salary scheme to new entrants.

Money-purchase pensions

If this is the case, the chances are you'll be offered either a 'money purchase' scheme, group personal pension or stakeholder pension.

The crucial difference is that you will have to buy an annuity with the fund you have built up, rather than be guaranteed a ratio of your salary. The value of your fund will depend largely on stockmarket conditions in the run up to your retirement. And although your employer will still contribute to the scheme, you'll need to take a much more active role in your pension affairs than if you had the luxury of a final-salary pension.

If your employer offers a group personal pension, he or she is obliged to contribute at least 3 per cent of your salary to the fund.

Group personal pensions are effectively a clutch of personal pensions bundled together, so when you leave an employer you can simply take your pension with you and can continue contributing to it.

What should you do with your pension when changing jobs?

The concept of a 'job for life' is well and truly extinct. Today's financial goddesses are not only likely to change jobs several times, but careers as well. They may well also spend time working abroad, or take time off to travel or do voluntary work.

If you're leaving a company pension scheme, start planning what you're going to do with the pension benefits at least *three months* before you're due to leave. Contact your personnel department. They will be able to give you full details of the benefits you have accrued and the fund's investments.

Then consider enlisting the help of a good pensions adviser to undertake an analysis of what to do next:

- Provided you've been contributing to the pension for at least two years, you can 'transfer' your pension to your new employer's scheme.
- However, you may well decide to leave your benefits invested in your ex-employer's fund, particularly if your pensions adviser deems it to be better than the one offered by your new employer.
- If you've been with your employer less than two years, you usually have to leave your pension behind.
- Keep records of all company pensions you build up but do not take with you in your 'housekeeping files'. Before you come to retire, you will need to get in touch with the personnel department of all these companies to draw your benefits.
- If you're leaving to become self-employed, or join a firm which does not offer a company scheme, you can transfer your benefits to a personal pension.

As discussed in the section on employee benefits in chapter 2, it is crucial to evaluate exactly what pension benefits your new employer offers. Do they contribute as much as your old employer? Will you be leaving behind a final-salary pension scheme for a money-purchase scheme?

Moving to a less generous pension scheme is tantamount to taking a pay cut. So, if you discover that changing jobs will entail taking a pension cut, negotiate a higher salary to make up for it.

Life-planning for your pension

As we said earlier, your pension is the backbone of your financial portfolio. Financial goddesses need to take two things into consideration when devising a pensions strategy. These are:

1) any spouse's pension they may be entitled to
2) how they are going to plug the pensions gap if they take a career break to have children.

Spouse's pension

If your husband is a member of a final-salary pension scheme, you will be entitled to a spouse's pension. But you're not entitled to any pension benefits if you're co-habiting.

Pensions are regarded as an asset in divorce, and they can be a rather large asset. It's not uncommon for lawyers to find that a divorcing man's pension can be worth considerably more than the family home, particularly if he's in his forties or fifties and has been saving hard.

Pension splitting on divorce

Traditionally in a divorce settlement, the husband walks away with the pension, and the wife with the family home and children. However, it is not uncommon for the husband's pension to be worth considerably more than the family home, particularly if he is a company director in his forties or fifties.

Therefore, pensions can be a major asset to be considered in divorce settlements. If you have been relying on your husband's pension to take care of you in your golden years, you'll need to start making provisions of your own after the divorce.

In December 2000, the government passed a new law on pension splitting which means that a woman divorcing her husband may be entitled to take a percentage of his pension at the time of the divorce, and invest it in her own personal pension.

Earmarking

Prior to that, the courts used a system known as earmarking, which meant that the husband could be ordered to designate a proportion of his pension for his ex-wife, through an attachment order. But this is messy. Not only does it prevent couples from making a clean break, it also means that if a woman's ex-husband died before retirement she would lose her pension benefits, or if she remarried, he could apply for the attachment order to be erased.

Pensions and babies

One of the main reasons why so many women retire on a smaller pension than their male counterparts is that when they stop work to have children, their pension contributions fall dramatically, and they therefore build up a smaller fund than someone who worked non-stop to the age of sixty.

If you are a member of a company scheme, your employer is obliged to maintain its proportion of contributions based on your salary while you are on paid maternity leave.

However, you are only required to make contributions based on your actual maternity pay. Let's look at how this works.

How much statutory maternity pay are you entitled to?

Provided you have been in continuous employment for at least twenty-six weeks before the qualifying period for maternity leave (i.e. the fifteenth week of pregnancy) you are entitled to twenty-six weeks' statutory maternity pay as follows:

- 90 per cent of your average earnings during the first six weeks' leave
- £100 a week, as of April 2003, for the remaining weeks.

Your employer may offer more generous maternity pay, but he/she is not legally obliged to.

As far as your pension goes, your employer is obliged to make the company's share of contributions based on your actual salary throughout the period of paid maternity leave. But as we said, you are only required to make contributions based on the actual maternity pay you receive.

So, say you earn £30,000, and your employer pays 8 per cent of your salary into your pension, and you pay 5 per cent:

- Your employer will continue paying £200 a month into your pension.
- However, you will only be required to pay 5 per cent of the average earnings you actually received in the first six weeks, then £5 a month based on the £100 flat rate during the remaining period.

Your employer is not required to make any pension contributions during *unpaid* maternity leave. So you can see how, even if a woman takes just two years off work, she will experience a pension shortfall.

Your thirties are an important period in your pensions cycle. With at least twenty years to go to retirement, you can afford to take considerable investment risk. So, if you can afford to make pension contributions of your own during maternity leave, this will certainly give your retirement fund a boost. If you cannot make increased contributions to your company scheme, you should take out a good stakeholder pension.

How will your pension grow?

The Financial Services Authority calculates that if a 25-year-old started saving £50 a month into a pension and increased her contributions in line with wage inflation (2 to 3 per cent), she could expect an income of about £310 a month at the age of sixty-five.

If she saved £100 a month, she would get £620. But if she delayed putting away £50 a month till she was thirty-five, she would get just £191 a month. At forty-five, it would fall to just £105 a month, and at fifty-five to £44.

These are estimated figures based on the pension fund growing by 7 per cent a year, but they give an idea of the cost involved in building up that elusive retirement pot, and the cost of delaying it.

The Inland Revenue currently levies a cap on the proportion of your income you can put into a pension:

- up to the age of thirty-five: 17.5 per cent of your earnings
- thirty-six to forty-five: 20 per cent of your earnings
- forty-six to fifty: 25 per cent of your earnings
- fifty-one to fifty-five: 30 per cent of your earnings.

However, since April 2001, even non-earners and children can save up to £2808 a year by taking out a 'stakeholder' pension, as explained below.

Counting the cost of inflation

Surfing the Internet, you'll find that many financial websites sport 'pension calculators'.

These can be helpful to calculate how much you need to start saving for your retirement. But it's important to factor in many variables, or your figures will be dangerously flawed.

The main thing to take into account is the effect of *inflation*. In thirty-two years' time, £2611 would be worth just £675.

By the same token, it's also important to increase your contributions in line with salary inflation. You'd be a bit miffed if your salary didn't go up one iota over ten years. So you need to increase your pension contributions in line with inflation, or your eventual retirement fund will be pretty worthless!

If inflation remained at 2.5 per cent a year, for the next twenty-five years, £1 of contributions today would be worth just 52p then. So, a 25-year-old, who starts saving £50 a month today, needs to increase her contributions in regular increments, to nearly £100 a month by the time she reaches fifty.

Investment growth and charges

Another factor to take into account is *investment growth*. Remember how, in the chapter on investments, we said you should aim for 8 per cent growth a year? Well sadly, many pension funds have been producing much less than that.

The other thing to look out for, is of course *charges*. The whole idea behind stakeholder pensions was to simplify the charging structure on personal pensions. But many old-style personal pensions are still hideously expensive. As well as having high running charges, they also levy punitive exit penalties, so not only will a large proportion of your contributions be eaten up by charges, you'll also be penalised if you stop contributions, or move to another fund.

Personal pensions

If you are self-employed, or your employer does not offer a company pension, but you want to take advantage of the tax relief offered on pensions, you'll have to take out a personal pension.

Stakeholder pensions

In an attempt to make pensions better value and encourage even non-earners to save for retirement, the government launched a new type of pension known as a stakeholder pension in April 2001.

The stakeholder pension is really just a low-cost personal pension. The maximum annual charge that can be levied on a stakeholder pension is capped at 1 per cent, and there can be no initial or set-up fee.

Most employers with five or more employees must offer access to a pension scheme through the workplace, and this could be a stakeholder scheme, though it does not have to be.

Pensions for children

The government's other 'big idea' when launching the stakeholder pension, was to make it available to non-taxpayers like children or non-earning wives, as well as earners. Non-earners can contribute up to £2808 a year into a stakeholder pension and receive tax relief on it.

Standard Life, a pensions provider, calculates that if parents made this maximum contribution on behalf of their child from birth to the age of twenty, the offspring could be guaranteed an income of about £26,000 a year from the age of sixty, even if the offspring in question never saved another penny towards their retirement in their adult years.

While the figures are compelling, you must remember that

under current rules your offspring would not be able to get their hands on the cash till they reach the age of fifty. As parents will undoubtedly have to pay much higher university tuition fees in future years, and most are finding funding their own pensions enough of a challenge, I'd have thought planning for their children's golden years would be the last thing on their minds.

Finally, employees who are members of a company pension scheme may also hold a stakeholder pension provided they do not earn more than £30,000 a year.

Alternatives to pensions

ISAs as pensions

The unfairness of the annuity system, and closure of final-salary schemes, is driving increasing numbers of investors to build up a retirement fund through a well-managed portfolio of ISAs, rather than pensions.

While the Inland Revenue offers tax relief on pension contributions, you must pay tax on your annuity income. However, as we said in the investment chapter, ISA investments roll up tax free. They are also yours to keep, and can be passed down to your heirs, rather than kept by annuity providers.

The maximum you can put into an ISA in any tax year is £7000, which equals £583.33 a month. That's a fair whack, but if you've no other savings or investments, that might not be enough to build up a decent pension and investments for university fees, holidays or home improvements.

So an increasing number of people are constructing their retirement fund though a mixture of ISAs and property.

Property as a pension

Over the past five years, property in central London has appreciated 103 per cent while the FTSE all-share index rose just 20 per cent.

But, of course, the real beauty of investing in property is that you are buying bricks and mortar, which will always have a physical value, and can be passed on to your children. Unlike a pension or ISA, property really is a tangible asset.

As we discussed in the last chapter, the idea of investing in property is that the rental income covers your mortgage payments and leaves you with a little profit, and that you also gain capital appreciation on the house when you come to sell.

A portfolio of investment properties can provide a great pension, because once you've paid off the mortgage, the rental income is yours to keep, or you can sell it and pocket a nice lump sum.

But you have to go about it carefully. A run of problem tenants will give you endless months of stress and could leave you in financial ruin, while a quirky flat miles away from anywhere may be impossible to let. So if you are thinking of investing in property, follow the rules:

1. Buy what will *let*, not what you like. Look for properties that will be easy to let and maintain, rather than simply places you'd personally like to live in.

   Location is paramount. Most renters are students, or young professionals who want to be close to transport and amenities. Avoid properties with gardens as they require constant maintenance, and they rarely add much to the property's rental value anyway. It's important to keep the property and furniture in good repair, or you'll only attract unemployed tenants.

2. Build up at least one year's mortgage payments as a cash

reserve. But the main thing to remember is that property is illiquid. If the stockmarket crashes you can usually cash in your investments and get your hands on the money within twenty-four hours, but it can take many months to sell a flat.

All landlords have void periods when they can't find tenants, and have to pay the mortgage, insurance, and maintenance costs out of their own pocket. For this reason, I would not recommend investing in property until you have built up at least one year's mortgage payments to dip into as a cash reserve.

3. Do your sums: letting agents, rent and mortgage. Managing tenants requires a lot more work than simply collecting the rent. You'll get calls in the middle of the night when a water pipe has burst or the central heating has packed in, and there's always the odd nuisance who can't change a light bulb, or simply runs away without paying the rent.

It's worth noting that the law really does seem to be on the tenants' side, rather than the landlord's. It's jolly difficult to get a problem tenant evicted.

So you may decide to appoint a lettings agent to take care of all that. Most will take 15 per cent of the rental income to find tenants and maintain the property, and even then there's no guarantee of it all being plain sailing.

4. Evaluate: is it worth it? So, say, you let a £100,000 flat for £800 a month. That's a gross rental income of £9,600 a year out of which you'll have to pay the mortgage, which at 4.85 per cent would come to £5,874.

If you appointed a lettings agent who took 15 per cent commission, that would shave another £1,440 off the gross income leaving you with just £2,286 a year profit. Out of this would have to come: insurance, service charges, maintenance costs, plus of course any void periods when you don't have tenants.

Working till you are seventy!

The thought of a whole new generation of bright young professionals retiring at sixty, and then spending twenty-five years' retirement does sound like a rather unworkable equation. So there's a new catchphrase going around the houses: seventy is the new fifty!

Whereas our parents aspired to retiring early, at fifty-five or even fifty, unless we're landed with a massive inheritance, or build up an unrealistically large pensions portfolio, that's unlikely to be a realistic option for us.

Indeed the question won't be can we afford to retire at fifty, but can we afford not to work till seventy?

8

Insurance and tax planning: take care of yourself

There's no point saving like a goddess, building up a fat retirement fund, and owning a palace, if you're not responsible enough to protect yourself, your loved ones and your assets.

While investment, property and pensions are about *building* wealth, insurance is about *protecting* your wealth should the worst happen. In short, it's about being responsible – the very antithesis of being apathetic! The key areas you need to insure are:

- your dependants and loved ones
- yourself
- your property and assets.

Financial goddesses learn what insurances they need, and how to shop for the best-value policies, early on in their lives.

If you're a student living away from home, you need to insure your possessions. If you have a car, you are required by law to take out insurance against injury and damage to other road users, and you may want extra breakdown cover for your vehicle. If you're going backpacking around the world and intend trying bungee-jumping, a bog-standard package holiday travel insurance policy won't cover you should the worst happen.

There's no point becoming a proud homeowner if you can't be bothered to insure the building and your contents in case of fire, flood or burglary. And if you have a family, your very first duty (even before you start saving and investing) is to ensure they'll be adequately protected should you become unable to work or die prematurely.

No financial goddess is negligent enough to skimp on the insurances she needs. Nor is she silly enough to buy a bundle of policies she doesn't need. If you and your husband have sufficient life insurance through your employer(s), don't let a bank manager talk you into buying some more. That's paying twice for something, and you've got better things to do with your money!

Life insurance

How much do you need?

Single women don't need life insurance. Mothers, with children under the age of eighteen who are financially dependent on them, certainly do.

To work out how much life insurance you need, calculate how much it would cost to pay off the mortgage, feed, clothe and look after your children and pay any school and university fees that come out of your salary, should you die.

If you don't work, calculate how much it would cost for your husband or partner to employ a replacement nanny. If you have children from a previous marriage and are still supporting them, calculate how much cover you need for them as well as your new family.

Most employers who offer life insurance offer cover worth three or four times an employee's salary. However, if you have a very large mortgage, or second family, you may well need to buy more.

How does life insurance work?

Life insurance pays out 'death benefits' to a beneficiary(s) if you die within a certain period. You can buy life insurance for a ten-, twenty- or thirty-year period. As parents today will undoubtedly have to fork out university tuition fees, you'll probably need at least twenty years' cover if you have a young family.

Avoid 'whole life' policies, or any investment-linked life insurances. These are expensive, and the 'investment' components are usually worthless. Just as it's important to keep your savings separate from your debts, you should keep your 'investments' (which are assets), separate from your insurances (which are protection).

The good news is that life insurance premiums have fallen dramatically in recent years. That's because we're apparently more likely to contract an illness or injury, and be laid up for months, than to snuff it completely! Yet R.J. Temple, an independent financial consultant, found that 20 per cent of people with families had no life insurance – and that, bizarrely, 24 per cent didn't know if they had any or not!

It also found that only 2 per cent of the families it surveyed had cover equivalent to more than fifteen years' earnings. Just as there's no point having a pension if you don't pay enough into it, there's no point having insurance if it doesn't cover you sufficiently. Below I outline the types of life insurance and how they work.

Decreasing term insurance

The cheapest form of life insurance is *decreasing term insurance*, which means the term over which you are insured decreases as you get older. This type of insurance is usually linked to your mortgage, so as you shave years off your mortgage, the period over which your life is insured falls too.

Decreasing term insurance is usually recommended as the cheapest and simplest way of buying life cover if you have a family. If you're both earning similar salaries, and share family bills more or less equally, it's worth buying a joint life policy which will cover both your lives for a single premium.

Family income benefit

An even cheaper form of cover than decreasing term insurance is *family income benefit*. This is often recommended for non-earning wives, but works equally well for earning women who employ nannies.

Whereas life insurance pays out a tax-free lump sum which your beneficiaries would have to manage, family income benefit pays a tax-free annual income until your children reach the age of eighteen or twenty-one. Obviously, this wouldn't pay off the mortgage in one clean sweep, but it would ensure enough income to pay for a nanny or housekeeper.

Single mothers and second families

If you divorce and take out your own mortgage, you must buy sufficient life insurance to cover the mortgage. If you are receiving maintenance from your ex-husband and want to protect this in the event of his untimely death, you can take out *confidential life insurance* on his life.

Ensure that the policies are correctly written, and that your beneficiaries know about them. Ignoring your responsibilities to children and spouses from previous marriages or relationships is not the behaviour of a financial goddess.

Write your insurance into a trust

You should also write your life insurance policy into a trust, so it is paid directly to your beneficiaries, and does not fall into your estate, when you die.

As we explained in chapter 2, if your assets (home, investments, etc.) are worth more than £250,000 when you die, your heirs will have to pay inheritance tax at 40 per cent on anything above that amount, unless you plan accordingly through wills and trusts.

Home insurance

You should ensure you have sufficient home insurance from the day you move into a new home. Many mortgage lenders will require you to have buildings insurance for the property you intend to buy, before advancing you the mortgage. But avoid lenders who insist you purchase your home insurance from them as part of the mortgage deal. The premiums are likely to be double or even triple the most competitive ones you'll find on the Internet.

There are two parts to home insurance: *buildings* insurance and *contents* insurance. It's best to buy a policy that combines the two, so in the event of a flood or fire, you only have to deal with one insurance firm.

Buildings insurance should cover the full cost of *rebuilding* your home (roof, walls, floors) and all fixtures like bathroom and kitchen units. The 'rebuild' cost is usually lower than the market value of the property. If you have a leasehold flat, the freeholder should insure the building of the entire block, and you only need to worry about insuring your contents.

Contents insurance covers possessions not fixed to your home: carpets, curtains, furniture, electrical items, clothes, artefacts, books. It's a good idea to maintain an ongoing list of possessions in your financial housekeeping file, as this will help if you do need to make a claim.

Keep the value of your cover under review. As a first-time buyer, the value of your possessions is likely to be low. But as you acquire new furniture and goods, you may need to increase your cover. Check for exclusions: expensive jewellery, antiques or musical instruments may not be covered, and will need to be insured separately.

Home insurance premiums are determined largely by postcode. So if you live in an area with a high crime rate, or risk of flooding, your premiums will be a lot higher than a safer area with less risk of natural disaster.

Ensure you comply with your insurer's requirements regarding safety locks on windows and doors, or it won't pay out in the event of a burglary. It may also refuse to pay out if you have left your home unoccupied for more than thirty days. As we said in chapter 3, some of the best home insurance deals are to be found online, with many insurers offering a discount for policies bought over the net.

Health insurance

Ideally every financial goddess would like fully comprehensive medical insurance that will cover her for major surgery, pregnancy, dental treatment, eye treatment, overseas health treatment, and a wide range of complimentary therapies at home and abroad. In reality, such luxury cover doesn't exist – and if it did, it would be prohibitively expensive.

Sophisticated advances in medical treatment mean private medical insurance (PMI) premiums have soared way above inflation in the past ten years, and are likely to continue rising.

Top-of-the-range comprehensive cover including alternative treatments and dental care for a healthy thirty-year-old could cost nearly £1000 a year. For a family of four, with both parents in their mid to late thirties, it could cost double that. As we said above, we're far more likely to suffer a major illness and survive, than die prematurely!

Benefits of private medical insurance

However, the benefit of PMI is that in an age of long NHS waiting lists, you'll have faster access to treatment – though in a real emergency like a heart attack, you'd be rushed to the nearest NHS hospital anyway.

But PMI plans come with a mind-boggling range of exclusions and caveats, which need to be considered carefully. You should also bear in mind that not all private hospitals have the same facilities as NHS ones. If complications were to arise, and the private hospital did not have consultants and equipment to hand, you might need to be transferred to an NHS hospital anyway.

Costs and complications of PMI

Because buying PMI can be expensive and complicated, you may well decide that you'd be better off building up investments and cash reserves. This way, you'll have the money to pay for private treatment if you need it, but won't have wasted your premiums if you don't.

An increasing number of insurers are now offering 'self pay' polices. In return for a nominal fee, you gain access to private hospitals and consultants, but pay for most or all of the treatment yourself.

BUPA was once the stalwart of the health insurance market, but has lost its lion's share, as other providers like PPP, Norwich Union and Standard Life have entered the fray. There are now over 150 different PMI policies available.

If you do decide to buy private medical cover, do your research. It might be worth consulting a financial adviser with a detailed knowledge of the market, but do bear in mind that they will probably earn commission on the policy they sell, so this may sway their recommendations.

Some things you should know about private health insurance:

1. What private medical cover will *not* include:
   - medical and hospital care during pregnancy. If you want to give birth in a private hospital you will have to pay for it yourself or through a 'self pay' policy
   - any existing medical conditions you have
   - drug or alcohol-related problems
   - psychiatric treatment, or AIDS
   - emergency treatment if you are involved in an accident. This is because in such an event you'd be rushed to the casualty/emergency department of the nearest NHS hospital anyway, though if you required a longer stay and had health insurance, you could ask to be transferred to a private hospital
   - chronic long-term illnesses.

2. What private medical insurance *can* cover, depending on the type of policy:
   - complications after pregnancy
   - alternative health treatments like osteopathy, acupuncture, homeopathy, reflexology or reiki, though you will usually have to be referred to a specialist by your GP. Some insurers still view complimentary therapies with scepticism
   - routine and major dental surgery
   - optical surgery
   - overseas surgery (if you're going skiing, surfing or scuba-diving, it's essential to buy winter/summer sports insurance)

- outpatient consultations.
3. Ways of keeping PMI premiums down:
    - buy a 'budget plan' which will only offer treatment for major surgery like cancer, heart surgery or a hip or knee replacement, which can cost anything upwards of £10,000
    - buy a policy with a high excess, so you pay the the first £100 or £250 of the bill. Most 'short-term' private treatments cost less than £5000
    - buy a plan which will only pay for treatment which you cannot receive on the NHS within 6 weeks
    - PMI plans offer different levels of accommodation, ranging from a 'hotel standard' room with TV and wine with meals, to a paid bed in an NHS hospital ward. The latter band will be cheaper than the former!

Travel insurance

Whether you're off on a idyllic painting holiday in France, trekking through the rainforests of Africa, or snowboarding in Aspen, you'll need travel insurance to cover you for delays and cancellations, emergency medical treatment, and repatriation.

Your travel insurance policy should cover:

- medical treatment and repatriation in the event of an accident or illness
- your luggage should it go missing or become damaged, and travel money that is lost or stolen
- compensation for delays, though insurers often impose excruciatingly long waiting times on the latter. An eight-hour wait for a charter flight is annoying but you're unlikely to receive compensation. However, if you're left stranded at the airport for more than twelve hours, you should receive something.

Types of cover

Do check if your credit card provider offers any cover if you purchase your holiday with it. If it doesn't, shop around for the cheapest quote.

If you travel frequently annual cover will be your cheapest bet. If you're going backpacking or scuba diving you'll need special cover.

Annual worldwide cover

If you frequently go away for last-minute breaks and take at least a couple of holidays a year, an annual worldwide policy will certainly work out cheaper and more practical than several separate policies.

Just as you shouldn't buy ISAs and pensions from your bank, you shouldn't buy travel insurance from a High Street travel insurance broker (or bank!) either. As always, some of the best value deals are to be found online.

An annual policy from a direct online provider for a single traveller can cost as little as £60 a year, for a family of four £80 a year. This will include winter sports and long-haul summer holidays.

Backpackers

If you're going off backpacking for several months, and planning to pick up casual work like fruit-picking or waitressing to fund your travels, a general travel insurance policy won't cover you should the worst happen.

Recent tragedies of young trekkers going missing in the rainforests of Australia and nightclubs of Tokyo mean backpackers' insurance costs have soared, and can be double or triple the cost of general annual worldwide cover. However, they can include many extras like cover when doing casual work, and even the cost of a return trip if you discover you need to rush back home to resit your exams!

Adventure sports

If you plan on engaging in a spot of mountaineering, heli-skiing, hang-gliding, or scuba-diving while you're on holiday, you'll need specialist cover. The insurer may impose strict conditions. If you're going scuba-diving, you may only be granted cover if you dive under supervision, or have a diving qualification.

Most insurers will require these activities to be 'incidental' and not the sole purpose of your trip. Also, they are unlikely to cover you for taking part in competitive sporting events, even if it is only for amateurs.

Finally!

Do remember to take your policy details with you, and make a note of any twenty-four-hour freephone numbers.

It's a good idea to send yourself an e-mail with details of your flight numbers, hotels, passport numbers and insurance details before you leave, so they are always at hand – provided of course you can find access to the Internet!

Car insurance

Women are deemed to be 'safer' drivers than men (they have the same number of accidents, but they tend to be of a less serious nature), so the financial goddess can make great savings on her motor insurance.

The law states that any driver must have insurance against injury or damage to a third party. However, many insurance policies offer much more than this. Comprehensive cover may include breakdown cover, legal expenses, insurance against theft or damage, and even the cost of a replacement hire car.

Your premiums will depend on: the type of vehicle you drive, your address, age and occupation. So, if you're a 24-year-old showbiz journalist driving a zippy new Mazda around central London, your premiums will be a lot higher than a 34-year-old science teacher running a Ford Fiesta in Sussex! Again, you'll find the best deals online, and may get a further discount if you buy your home and motor cover from the same insurer.

Ways of reducing your car insurance premiums:

- take the advanced driving test
- build up a no-claims bonus
- if you're a couple, and share a car, insure it in your name.

Most British insurance policies will cover you when driving in the EU, but usually only for third party cover, so if you take the car to France it might be worth buying extra breakdown cover.

Tax planning

There's a well-worn saying that we can only be certain of two things in life: death and taxes.

Nobody likes paying more tax than they should, so the canny financial goddess will ensure she grasps every opportunity to reduce her tax bill. However, there's a fine line between tax *avoidance* and tax *evasion*. The former is honest, legal and a good financial-planning strategy. The latter is not, and can even lead to imprisonment!

We can't include every tax saving tip in this book. However, the guide below explains the different taxes you may have to pay, and also two new tax credits for lower earners and families, which came into force in April 2003.

What is tax?

We'll look at three different types of tax here:

- income tax
- National Insurance
- capital gains tax.

As the term suggests, income tax is the tax you pay on any income you derive from employment, investments or property.

The level of income tax you pay depends on how much you earn. However, we all have a *personal allowance* – the amount we can earn without paying tax. Anything over this is taxed at three different rates.

For the tax year April 2003–2004, the rates are:

- personal allowance: £4615
- the next £1,960 (taking your income up to £6,575) is taxed at 10 per cent
- the following £18,540 (anything over £6,575) is taxed at 22 per cent
- anything over £35,115 is taxed at 40 per cent.

So, if you earned £25,000, you would:

- earn £4,615 tax-free
- pay 10 per cent tax on the next £1,960
- and 22 per cent tax at the next £18,425
- bringing your total annual tax bill to £4,053.50.

National Insurance

On top of income tax, you also pay National Insurance (NI). As we explained in the pensions chapter, NI is used to pay for social security contributions. But you need the mind of a genius to understand exactly how National Insurance works. For our purposes, it's sufficient to say National Insurance is another form of income tax.

There are four different classes of NI contributions. If you are employed, your NI contributions are deducted from your salary together with your income tax, and paid by your employer. If you are self-employed, you pay your NI contributions with your tax bills.

Capital gains tax

Any gains you make from the sale of investments (outside an ISA) or property (other than your main residence) over £7,900 is subject to capital gains tax at your highest rate.

So, if you bought an investment flat for £100,000 and sold it for £200,000 eight years later, you might have to pay capital gains tax (CGT) on the profits made. This is something to bear in mind if you do decide to invest in property.

If you have a large share portfolio, it's worth keeping an eye on the profits. If the shares have soared in value, it might be worth selling some of them, to avoid rolling up CGT liability in future years.

Bed and breakfasting

However, if you don't wish to sell because the time isn't right, you can roll up a CGT liability by selling your shares in one tax year (just before 4 April) and then buying them back more than thirty days later in the following tax year. This is known as bed and breakfasting.

You may wish to buy back the shares within an ISA, and protect yourself from incurring any further tax liability. But remember, you will have to pay brokers' costs and stamp duty on your share dealing, and there will also be a fee for the ISA wrapper. Also, remember you can only take out one equity ISA in any tax year.

How do you pay tax?

When you start your first job, you'll be given a form P46, so your employer can pay tax on your behalf through the pay-as-you-earn (PAYE) scheme. The Inland Revenue may also send you a P91 to fill in, to ensure you are paying the right amount.

Tax code

You'll be given a tax code. The first step to ensuring you aren't paying too much (or too little!) tax is to make sure your tax code is correct.

Accountants reckon that 10 per cent of tax codes are wrong, and that the figures can be incorrect by up to 30 per cent. You may pay too much tax if for some reason you are given an 'emergency tax code'. However, this is usually rebated the day after your employer gets a proper tax code.

Taxable benefits

You should also be aware of any benefits which you may be taxed on. As we said earlier in this chapter, you will have to pay tax on health insurance premiums your employer makes on your behalf.

Company cars are also a taxable benefit. The amount you have to pay will depend on the price of the car and the number of business miles you clock up. Since April 2002, cars emitting less carbon dioxide are taxed more favourably.

What to do when leaving a job

When you leave a job, you'll get a P45. It's important to hand this to your new employer, or you could end up paying too much tax when you start your new job. If you don't go on to another job, or claim benefits, contact the Inland Revenue with your P45, as you may be entitled to a repayment.

Self-assessment

If you are self-employed, a higher-rate tax payer, company director, or have income from letting property, you'll need to fill in a self-assessment tax return. This must be completed and returned to the Inland Revenue by 31 January after the tax year ends, or you will be subjected to a fine of £100.

The first self-assessment forms were issued in April 1997. The idea behind self-assessment is that your tax is worked out on the figures you provide, without the Inland Revenue checking them in detail first.

If you want the Inland Revenue to calculate your tax bill for you, fill it in and submit it to them, before *31 September* of the following tax year. If you, or your accountant, work out the bill, simply pay the amount you calculate is due, when you file your return by 31 January.

Reducing your tax bill

As we discussed in the chapters on saving and investment, we all have an ISA allowance of £7000 (maxi ISAs), or £3000 a year (two mini ISAs).

By lodging spare cash into an ISA, it will grow tax free. However, interest earned on savings accounts and investment outside ISAs will be taxed at your relevant rate. If you are a non-taxpayer, fill in form R98 to get the tax rebated.

Self-employed people should ensure they claim all the business expenses they are entitled to.

As of April 2003, if you are on a low income, or have children and a joint income of less than £58,000, there are two tax credits you may be eligible to claim, which will leave you with more money in your pocket.

Working families tax credit

As of April 2003, couples and single people on a low income, who work at least sixteen hours a week, may benefit from working tax credit.

The credit is means-tested and comprises a basic element of £29.90 a week plus various other extras for lone parents, those who work more than thirty hours a week, and disabled people.

There is also a 'childcare element'. The maximum credit for one child is £135 a week, for two children £200 a week.

The basic element is paid through your employer and deducted from your tax bill. So, if you pay £40 in tax a week, and are entitled to £20 a week working tax credit, your bill will be reduced to £20 a week. However, just to make matters complicated, the childcare element is paid directly to the main carer, rather than through your pay slip.

Child tax credit

On top of child benefit, which is paid to all parents with children under nineteen in full-time education, irrespective of how much they earn, households with a combined income of less than £58,000 a year (but no more than £42,450 for any one parent) are eligible for child tax credit.

Child tax credit comprises a family element of £10.24 a week, which is paid to all qualifying families falling under the threshold, plus a 'child element' of up to £27.75 per child. The 'child element' is means-tested, and like the child element of the working tax credit, child tax credit is paid directly to the main carer.

Working out how much credit you may be entitled to is fiendishly complicated. Don't expect a financial adviser to be able to explain it to you. If you don't have an accountant, visit your local Citizens Advice Bureau, which will have trained advisers able to explain exactly what tax credits you may be eligible for, and how to apply for them.

9

Financial goddesses
are made not born

This aim of this book is to encourage you to take control of your hard-earned cash, create wealth and achieve financial security and independence.

As we have explained, this requires *planning* from your early twenties to your golden years, and ensuring you have sufficient intake of the *five core financial vitamins*: savings, investments, mortgages, retirement funds and insurances, at each life stage.

Although we've given several scenarios, we haven't by any means covered everything. No book could do that. Every woman is different and has different financial needs. If you're a professional violinist, you'll want to insure your instrument with specially underwritten cover. If you run your own business, you may want to investigate self-invested-personal pensions (SIPPs) that allow you to borrow money tax free from your pension fund to buy business premises. If you're landed with an unexpectedly large inheritance or bonus, you might want to look at lodging some of it offshore. If you work abroad for more than six months of the year, you may need special tax advice. These are specialist financial areas that go beyond the scope of this book, and require good professional advice.

Practice makes perfect

You may at this stage be wondering how my own finances fare. Do I save? When I can. Have I found the best mortgage? Yes, I think so. Have I achieved a balance between spending and saving? More or less. Do I have a pension? No. Have I bought and sold my investments at the right time? I'm working on it! Why am I telling you all this? To illustrate the point that financial goddesses are made not born!

It took me quite a while to get around to changing my bank account. I really ought to get some of my investments online, and I'm sure I could save a few pounds on my home insurance if I surfed the Internet.

I hope this book has demonstrated just how *easy* it is to start taking control of your money. Building wealth and achieving financial security isn't difficult, nor does it depend on chance and luck. But it *does* require practice!

Financial goddesses develop over time, not overnight

Becoming a financial goddess is all about achieving a balance between spending and saving, honing your budgeting and investing skills, and keeping your finances under review. For most women, this is an attitude that develops over time, not overnight. If you've been a shopaholic all your life and never saved a penny, you'll need to train yourself to exercise control.

Try this. Next time you get the urge to buy a new pair of shoes, lipstick, book, whatever, even though you've got cupboards full of them at home already, force yourself to walk away, promising that'll you'll come back in a day or two, if you still want or need them.

It's funny, but if you're a real 'impulse shopper' who just goes for the 'quick retail fix' to cheer yourself up, chances are you won't even *remember* the items the next day (because you'll have moved on to something else)! Giving yourself time to reflect enables you to differentiate between what you really need and want, and what's simply an impulse buy. And that's the first step to shopping like a goddess.

Watch your savings *grow* in a jam jar

Still need more incentive? Then put the money you save by *not* succumbing to impulse into a big fat glass jar, and keep that jar somewhere prominent and visible (like the top of your fridge).

I started doing this when I realised that I was spending a disproportionate amount of money (and time!) working in cafés. On average, I'd spend £5 to £6 on coffees and sandwiches, often costing me more than £100 a month! So I decided to limit myself to two trips a week (and collect loyalty cards at Starbucks and Coffee, etc., so I get a free coffee after a number of visits!). I put the £10 a week I've saved into the jar. Watching all those notes build up is a delightful incentive to keep going – and (you've probably guessed this bit's coming next) if I keep it up for a year, I'll have accumulated £520!

So don't think you simply weren't born with the 'knack' of managing money well, just because your finances have been a bit haphazard so far. Every woman can transform herself from an apathetic financial duckling to a wealth-building financial goddess. And every woman deserves the confidence that comes with knowing she can afford to live for a few months if she lost her job or fell ill. That she can save herself thousands of pounds over a lifetime on her mortgage, and that she is building up investments and retirement plans that will take care of her in her twilight years.

Review your financial CV

We're getting to the end now, so it's time to see how much you've learnt. In chapter 2, we asked you to write your financial CV. If you've been working through this book chapter by chapter, pull out your CV again now, and look at it afresh, with your financial-goddess eyes. How does it look now that you've acquired new financial skills?

Put your goddess-like savvy into *action*

Can you spot 'dud' investments that are eating away at your hard-earned cash? Or have you got pensions you haven't put a single penny into for years? Do you have enough insurance? Are you paying over the odds on your mortgage? What are you going to do about it?

If you've got too much money sitting around in cash, why not start directing some of it into an investment by setting up a monthly savings plan? If you're still trying to save while paying off debts, stop reading, turn back to chapter 3, and start clearing your debts *before* you start saving!

Just as enrolling at a new gym without ever working out there isn't going to make you fit, digesting an entire book on budgeting, saving, investing and insuring without actually making any changes to your finances isn't going to make you rich! So start putting some of your newly acquired goddess-like savvy into action now.

Do you need a financial adviser?

If you get a buzz out of comparing financial products, and are happy to take care of all the administration of applying for mortgages, pensions and investments, you may never need a financial adviser.

As we've said before, the growth of online finance means consumers today have almost as much information at their fingertips as the experts. You can research and buy investments, mortgages and insurances over the net, as easily as you can last-minute flights and hotels. But if your financial affairs are quite complicated, or you still lack confidence, you may decide to consult a financial adviser.

I often think the term 'financial adviser' is a bit misleading, as 'advisers' who are tied to a bank or insurance firm can only recommend products sold by those firms. And, more often than not, even the so-called 'independent' financial advisers are not as independent as they could be! Ultimately, only you can decide if you need to see a financial adviser. However, if you are in any of the situations below, it might be worth considering:

- You have dependants and your estate is worth more than £250,000.
  You should obtain advice on inheritance tax planning, either through a specialist financial adviser, lawyer or accountant.
- You have a very large inheritance or bonus to invest.
  You can come up with an investment strategy yourself, but it might be worth 'bouncing off' ideas with a good investment adviser. If you've used your ISA allowance and can tie up the money for several years, it might be worth investing offshore.
- You believe you may have been missold an endowment, pension or investment.
  The last thing you feel like doing is seeing *another* financial adviser, but a good one may help guide you through

the bureaucratic rigmarole of applying for compensation.
- You want specific advice on the best health insurance policy for you or your family, want to set up a sophisticated pension scheme, or are changing jobs but unsure how to evaluate the benefits package.

You need to find an adviser who specialises in that particular area, not just a generalist.

How to find a good financial adviser

This really is the million-dollar question. Obviously you're not going to find the best financial adviser by flicking through the *Yellow Pages*. You should also be wary of people giving out leaflets at stations or shopping malls, or placing small ads in glossy magazines. All good businesses advertise from time to time, but they don't reduce to touting, like ambulance-chasing personal injury firms.

Likewise, it's worth bearing in mind that many of the 'experts' regularly quoted in the financial press are really just using the media to drum up more business. Most have some degree of merit, or presumably journalists wouldn't contact them in the first place. But don't believe that they're the crème de la crème of the industry by any means, and certainly don't take everything they say as gospel!

Finding a really good financial adviser is hard, and it may take some time. If you've received bad advice in the past, you may have completely lost faith in the industry. You may also be due compensation; if so, follow the guide later in this chapter on how to make a financial complaint.

Six steps to finding a good financial adviser
1. Tied or independent?
   The first thing to establish is whether the adviser is 'tied' or 'independent'. Tied financial advisers can only recommend products sold by the particular insurance or

investment house or bank they are 'tied' to. Advisers must disclose if they are tied to a particular firm before making recommendations. Unless you believe the firm really does offer the best value and performance over all others (unlikely, but I'm willing to give anyone a fair go), tied advisers are best avoided.

Independent financial advisers (IFAs) can sell products from a wide range of investment houses, insurance companies, banks and building societies. Their job is constantly to comb the market for the best-performing investments and pensions and best value mortgages and insurances. But how well they do this, will depend on their knowledge and experience of the market. It may also be swayed by how much *commission* they receive.

2. Fee or commission based?

The second decision to make is whether to opt for a fee-based or commission-based adviser.

Financial advisers make their living through their clients. That's fair enough. They earn their keep by either charging their clients an hourly or fixed *fee*, or by earning *commission* on what they sell. Some advisers offer clients the option of fee- or commission-based advice, or a mixture.

There is a view out there that fee-based advisers have more of an incentive to offer 'independent' advice and tackle financial-planning strategies, because they are being paid for their time, and not for what they sell. Advisers who work on commission are only too aware that they won't earn anything unless you actually buy a product from them, so you may find that your consultation comprises little more than a series of investment or insurance recommendations.

If you do opt for commission-based advice, ask the IFA how much commission they will earn from the sale. Some advisers may rebate a percentage of the commission they earn back to you, and they certainly shouldn't show offence at being asked how much they'll make.

3. Check that your adviser is properly qualified.

All independent financial advisers (IFAs) must be registered with the Financial Services Authority (FSA) – the regulatory body for the UK financial services industry.

If an adviser is not registered, he or she cannot legally sell financial products, and if you are missold a product, you won't be protected by the Financial Ombudsman Service (explained below). You can check if an adviser is registered by logging onto the FSA website (www.fsa.gov.org) and searching the central register of IFAs. Or you can call the register number.

All IFAs must have passed three levels of the Financial Planning Certificate. Some IFAs may hold the Advanced Planning Certificate, and investment specialists may hold the Investment Advisers Certificate. However, while these qualifications show that the adviser has attained a certain degree of knowledge about financial regulation, investments and the financial services market, the only real way to establish if an adviser is right for *you* is by meeting them.

4. Where to look for an adviser.

Do ask friends, family, or even your employer if they can recommend an adviser who has done a good job for them. Otherwise two bodies, IFA Promotion and the Personal Investment Authority, maintain lists of financial advisers up and down the country.

I have on occasion flicked through IFA Promotion's handbook to find an adviser who specialises in a specific area like offshore finance, or pensions, and called them up, but I can't say I've been that impressed by the insipid advice they provided. Still, if you need an adviser with expertise in a particular area, like employee benefits, health insurance, estate planning or complex pension schemes, call up one or both of these bodies and ask for some names.

Then call the firms direct. Outline briefly how you hope they may be able to help you. Ask them how long they have specialised in their particular area. If you have received bad advice in the past, will they help you apply for compensation ? What is their complaints procedure? If you like what you hear, set up an initial consultation.

5. Good things to ask a financial adviser at your consultation. All advisers (and accountants) will offer a free consultation before you hand over your affairs to them, so have a list of specific questions to take with you to the meeting, like: I want to invest in ISAs for school fees, what strategy would you suggest? Or, I want to buy health insurance that will cover dental treatment and osteopathy, what are the best options?

Meeting a financial adviser is a bit like a blind date; you don't know anything about them but may be about to hand over your finances to them! So it's vital that you feel *comfortable* discussing your financial affairs with them, and that you're roughly on the same *wavelength*.

As we've said before, there's no 'right' or 'wrong' way to invest a £5000 lump sum. Five different advisers could come up with five different strategies. You need to decide which one sounds best for you. Having questions prepared shows you're in control of your money and will keep the advisers on their toes!

Finally, if an adviser displays any kind of irritation when you quiz them on their suggestions, or ask them about commission, or they just can't come up with a good enough rationale for why they have recommended a particular product, take your business elsewhere.

6. And what should you expect your financial adviser to do? When a financial adviser takes you on as a client, he or she

should conduct a full *fact find* to determine your financial goals and attitude to risk. This is quite similar to the financial CV you drew up in chapter 2. It should take at least an hour for them to build up a full picture. In addition, you should expect your financial adviser to be accommodating on the following points:

- Why did you sell me that?
  Your adviser should provide a written explanation as to *why* they recommended a particular product.
- What's it all about? You should also receive a *key features* document detailing the aims, benefits and risks of the products you are sold.
- It's not right for me after all.
  You must be given a *cooling off* period should you decide you don't actually want a product after all.
- I'm not happy with the way I have been treated.
  You should also be given a copy of the firm's *complaints procedure*.

The problem with financial advisers

As I said, I'm willing to give anyone a fair go, but I have to say, in my years of writing financial makeovers, I've been largely disappointed with the quality of the financial advisers I've dealt with.

Very few were able to think laterally. Most were inclined to simply chuck over a few suggestions for ISAs, pensions or mortgages, which they'd recommended a hundred times before, without giving real thought and analysis to the person's financial situation. When they did suggest investments or mortgages, they rarely mentioned all the charges, until I prodded them. As we've stressed so many times throughout this book, you really do need to view a product as a complete picture, with all its exit penalties and costs, before you can evaluate how good it is for your portfolio.

Financial advisers aren't 'magicians' who can wave a wand and make you rich overnight. As we've said, most of them make a large percentage of their earnings through *selling* financial products, rather than coming up with planning strategies. A good relationship with an expert financial adviser could help you achieve your financial goals, but it might take time and work to find the right 'financial angel'!

How to make a financial complaint

The more knowledge you acquire about banks, investments, consumer rights and financial advisers, the less likely it is you'll have to make a financial complaint. But even the most canny financial goddess might get caught out, so you need to know the correct procedure for making a financial complaint.

Has the firm broken its own code?

Most banks, mortgage lenders and insurance companies volunteer to be bound by the 'banking' code, 'mortgage' code or 'insurance' code. It's a good idea to obtain copies of these codes from the relevant bodies and keep them in your financial housekeeping file for future reference. For example, the banking code sets out how banks should advise customers of rate changes, and treat customers who fall into debt.

One of the first steps in determining if you have a genuine financial complaint, is to check if the firm has broken its respective code. If you can prove that it has and in what way, it will certainly strengthen your case.

Contact the firm in the first instance

If you're unhappy with the way you have been treated by a bank, investment or insurance company, contact the person who dealt with you in the first instance. You can call, but it's best to put your query in writing. It's important to understand what constitutes a genuine financial complaint, and what doesn't.

If you have suffered financial loss as a result of a bank, financial adviser or insurance company's wrongdoing – e.g. been overcharged interest on a credit card, loan or overdraft, sold an endowment, investment or pension without being fully informed of the charges and risks involved, then you have cause for complaint. But if you're simply disappointed that an investment has not performed as well as you hoped, you do not!

Mistakes do happen. If you're concerned about a figure or calculation that appears on a statement, write to the person concerned and ask them for an explanation. This gives them the opportunity to put things right if they have made a mistake, and many discrepancies are sorted out this way.

If the matter remains unresolved, write again, but this time address your letter to the most senior person within the organisation. Head your letter 'complaint', and explain that the person who dealt with you was unable to resolve your problem. Order your points logically and stick to the facts. Say what you wish the organisation to do about your complaint, but don't use emotional, abusive or sarcastic language. It reduces your credibility and even could end up hampering your case.

If the firm refuses to engage in the matter any further – as has been the case with many mortgage holders who were missold endowments in the mid to late eighties – you need to contact the Financial Ombudsman Service (FOS).

The Financial Ombudsman

The Financial Ombudsman offers a free, independent service for resolving disputes between consumers and the financial services industry. It covers banks, building societies, mortgage lenders, insurance companies and credit card companies, but not personal loans taken out by firms other than banks or building societies, or mortgage or general insurance brokers.

The FOS operates under the Financial Services Authority (FSA). Its remit is to seek redress on behalf of consumers it believes have suffered financial loss. To this end, it has the power to order firms to pay compensation of up to £100,000 in the case of financial wrongdoing.

But don't get too excited. In reality most awards are quite small, and each case is taken on its individual merit. So just because someone suffers a similar dispute to yourself and receives damages, it does not mean that you automatically will too.

Fill in the FOS's complaints form

To lodge a complaint with the Ombudsman, you'll need to fill in a complaints form which can be downloaded from the FOS website (www.financial-ombudsman.org.uk) or obtained by calling the office. Again, you should enclose all necessary documentation.

The FOS reckons it can settle most cases within four months, and as we said above, it will cost you nothing. However, many endowment victims have had to wait up to a year for their cases to be settled, and not all have received the compensation they deserve.

What to do if you were missold an endowment

As we've discussed in previous chapters, endowment policies are stockmarket-linked investments which can go up and down in value.

They were oversold in the eighties on the premise that provided the policy achieved the projected growth rate (anything from 6 to 9 per cent), it would pay off the capital value of your home. But as many victims have found out to their cost, there's no guarantee of this, and there may well be a considerable *shortfall* in the amount you borrowed to buy your home and the value of your endowment when it matures. If you were not informed of these risks at the point of sale, you were missold the product, and should seek redress.

Just how bad is the problem?

As stockmarkets plummet, the endowment crisis deepens. More than 60 per cent of endowment policies aren't on track to pay off their policyholders' mortgages, and some policy holders are facing a shortfall of £10,000 or more.

In December 2002, the FSA fined Abbey Life (a subsidiary of Lloyds TSB) £1m, for widespread misselling of endowments over a five-year period. The insurer was forced to pay compensation totalling £160m to 50,000 customers. Further fines were believed to be in the pipeline at the time, but the FSA has been criticised for downplaying the endowment scandal and due to a regulatory loophole not all victims will receive the compensation they deserve.

Were you sold the policy before April 1988?

As we said above, your first port of call, if you believe you were missold a policy, is the adviser who sold you the product. If they have closed down or disappeared, you need to get in touch with the insurance company itself. If they are unwilling to play ball, the next step is to complain to the Ombudsman.

However, if you were sold the policy before April 1988 and cannot trace the firm that sold the policy, or get any joy from the insurance company, there is nothing the FSA can do to help, because the sale took place before new financial regulations and safeguards were introduced. If you fall into this miserable trap, there's nothing more you can do to seek the compensation you deserve, except launch an expensive and lengthy legal battle at your own cost.

So how effective is the regulator?

All this begs the question, just how effective is the regulator? The FSA has come under heavy criticism from the media and pressure groups for downplaying the severity of the endowment misselling scandal, and also for its failure to protect consumers during the collapse of Equitable Life, Britain's largest mutual insurer.

In 2000, Equitable Life lost a court battle with policyholders over guaranteed pensions, and was forced to close itself off from new business. At the time, insurance companies came under the regulation of the Treasury (the FSA only became a super-regulator with responsibility for all different areas – banks, insurers, investment houses, etc – in November 2001).

However, although the Treasury was aware of Equitable Life's financial problems *before* it lost its court case, it failed to protect consumers properly, because it allowed Equitable to continue soliciting for new business.

Furthermore, after Equitable had lost its case and closed off to new business, many of its existing policyholders (who included high-profile newsreaders and financial journalists), who would have been better off withdrawing their money at the earliest opportunity and investing it elsewhere, were encouraged instead to remain with the ailing insurer. Financial advisers complained that the FSA made it difficult for them to recommend that policyholders move their money to a more secure insurer, and many lost thousands of pounds as a result. So although regulation is in place to protect the consumer, it's not foolproof, as there isn't really anyone who regulates the regulator.

The financial goddess in relationships

This book is all about achieving financial independence. However, most financial goddesses will, at some point, merge finances either with a live-in partner or husband.

While two good incomes will certainly enable you to enjoy a better quality of life, and share bills as well as housework, it's a sad fact of modern life that marriages do break down. In Britain, a staggering 40 per cent of marriages end in divorce, which is jolly lucrative work for lawyers.

So, at the risk of finishing off on a melancholy note, this book ends with a guide to protecting your finances in a relationship, and managing your finances through, and after, a divorce. Even if your marriage or relationship is strong enough to stand the test of time, a sudden change in either partner's financial circumstances, can rock a few boats.

Friction can occur if, say, your boyfriend or husband earns substantially more and so always buys dinner or holidays, then suddenly loses his job or decides to jack it in to go freelance, and it falls on you to pick up the tab, or vice versa. Similarly, if one partner's income suddenly shoots up, they may start to resent having to support the lower-earning partner.

Protect yourself from STDs (sexually transmitted debts)

But much more worrying than that is the coterie of sad men who live off their partner's money like parasites, and run her into debt and financial ruin.

Remember, if you take out a joint mortgage, bank account or credit card, you are both jointly liable for loans. If one of you defaults on repayments or goes on a shopping spree, the lender or bank can pursue the other. This is why mortgage lenders prefer lending to couples rather than singles!

If you are thinking of moving in with a new partner, protect yourself from STDs (sexually transmitted debts), by retaining *separate* bank accounts and credit cards for your personal salaries and spending. If you're co-habiting rather than getting married, rent for a few months before buying.

Protecting your finances if you are co-habiting

English law does not offer co-habiting couples the same rights as married couples. So if you set up home with a partner without getting married, it might be worth drawing up a co-habitation agreement. Like a pre-nuptial agreement, this sets out how you will divide your assets if you do part company. Research shows that live-in relationships are even more likely to end in a split than marriages, presumably because it's a lot easier to separate. Some issues you may wish to address are:

Property
The most bitter battles that erupt when couples split are those concerning property. If you move into a partner's home but don't pay anything towards the mortgage, you won't be entitled to any interest in the property if you do separate, even if you've spent years raising children from the relationship. Although courts may allow you to remain in the family home while your child is growing up, you could find yourself out on the street when your youngest child turns eighteen, so think carefully before entering into such an arrangement.

If you buy a property together, you should treat it in the same way you would if buying with a girlfriend. Implement a 'trust deed' at the time of purchase, so you each own the percentage of the home you have bought, and have the right to buy the other out if you split up. If you're renting, ensure that both your names are on the tenancy agreement.

Children
If you or your partner have children from a previous marriage or relationship and are paying maintenance, it can put stress on a new relationship. So discuss exactly how you will organise your finances before moving in together.

Are you willing to pay a larger share of the mortgage if your partner has maintenance to pay? If you are bringing children from a previous marriage or relationship into a new one, will your new partner help support them?

Is there sufficient insurance in place should the worst happen? If you bought a joint endowment, you'll have to decide whether you keep it going even though you are no longer living together, trade it on the secondhand market or cash it in.

Tying the knot

It's not worth getting married for tax benefits these days. The married couple's tax allowance was scrapped in 2001. However, marriage does offer a certain amount of security and stability, particularly if you have children.

Paying for a wedding is an expensive business, and the same rules that apply to shopping apply here: plan, stick to a budget, and haggle! If you're marrying out of season, e.g. autumn/winter, you'll find it easier to negotiate reception hall fees, etc., than if you're getting married in the spring or summer. Ditto, marquee hire, caterers, etc.

That's the fun stuff. But day-to-day and long-term finances need to be planned and discussed too. Fish out your financial CV, and get your partner to compile one too. If you're retaining separate bank accounts and credit cards, you can have your own budgets for personal spending, but you should set up a joint savings account to pay for household bills, furniture, holidays and Christmas. If one of you is a higher-rate taxpayer, and the other a lower-rate taxpayer, a joint savings account allows you to reduce tax by channelling interest earned to the lower-rate payer. You should also pack away money for the long term by using your joint ISA allowance of £14,000 a year, and take out life insurance.

Pre-nuptial agreements have become fashionable ever since Catherine Zeta-Jones and Michael Douglas signed one. Like co-habitation agreements, this sets out what assets you will be entitled to should the marriage end in divorce. Not romantic, but it will serve a purpose if the worse does happen, I guess.

Divorce

If you've always relied on your husband to take care of the mortgage, investments, pensions and insurance, and the marriage ends in divorce, or you end up a widow, it can induce those negative feelings of fear and ignorance that we discussed at the beginning of the book.

So take a deep breath, and think about how you're going to plan for the short, medium and long term. Everyone – husband, wife and kids – ends up poorer as a result of a divorce. But many women lose more, because they're unaware of the pension benefits they could be signing away. The only people who make money are the lawyers, so the more arrangements you can settle between yourselves, the better.

The family home
Again, the first battle ground is usually the family home. If one of you can't afford to buy the other out, or pay two mortgages, you'll have to sell the property and each buy smaller places.

After sorting out who's getting the DVD player and who's taking the antique dresser, work out a financial plan for your new future. Insure your home, pay off your credit card debts and start saving. If divorce means you have less disposable income than when you were married, turn back to chapter 4 and find ways of trimming your day-to-day spending.

Invest for the future
Going through a divorce can be traumatic. Still, it's fascinating to see just how resourceful it can make some women.

One lady who divorced in her mid-forties decided to invest in property for her pension. She remortgaged her home to put down a 20 per cent deposit on a small council house near a university in south London, and rented it out to a group of student girls.

The house soared in value, so a couple of years later, she remortgaged that to put down a deposit on another place in the same area, and then another place. In twenty years' time, when she's paid off the three mortgages (which are being taken care of by the rent) and sold the properties (which no doubt, will have appreciated even more) she'll be a millionairess!

She wasn't particularly rich, or a gambler. But she was prepared to do a bit of research, take on a bit of debt to invest, and spend a few hours a week taking care of the administration, to provide for herself in her golden years. If she can do it, you can!

Appendix

Useful addresses and websites

Consumer advice, complaints and regulatory bodies

Association of British Insurers
51 Gresham Street
London EC2V 7HQ

Tel: 0207 600 3333
website: www.abi.org.uk

British Bankers' Association (for dormant accounts and banking code)
Pinners Hall
105–108 Old Broad Street
London EC2N 1EX

Tel: 0207 216 8800
website: www.bba.org.uk

Mortgage Code Compliance Board (for mortgage code)
University Court
Stafford ST18 OGN

Tel: 01785 218200
website: www.mortgagecode.org.uk

Financial Services Authority (FSA)
25 The North Colonnade
Canary Wharf
London E14 5HS

Tel: 0845 606 1234
website: www.fsa.gov.uk

Financial Ombudsman Service
South Quay Plaza
183 Marsh Wall
London E14 9SR

Tel: 0845 080 1800
website: www.financialombudsman.org

Office of Fair Trading
Fleetbank House
2-6 Salisbury Square
London EC4Y 8TX

Tel: 08457 224499
website: www.oft.gov.uk/consumer

Savings and investment clubs

ProShare UK (for investment clubs)
Centurion House
24 Monument Street
London EC3R 8AQ

Tel: 0207 220 1730
website: www.proshare.org

National Savings
Glasgow G58 1SB

Tel: 0845 964 5000
website: www.nationalsavings.co.uk

Credit Reference Agencies

Experian
Consumer Help Service
PO Box 9000
Nottingham NG80 7WP

Tel: 0870 241 6212
website: www.experian.co.uk

Equifax
Credit File Advice Centre
PO Box 1140
Bradford BD1 5US

Tel: 08705 143700
website: www.equifax.co.uk

Financial advisers

Society of Financial Advisers
20 Aldermanbury
London EC2V 7HY

Tel: 0208 989 8464
website: www.sofa.org

IFA Promotion
2nd Floor
117 Farringdon Road
London EC1R 3BX

Tel: 0800 085 3250
website: www.unbiased.co.uk

Unclaimed assets

Unclaimed Assets Register
Leconfield House
Curzon Street
London W1J 5JA

Tel: 0870 241 1713
website: www.uar.co.uk
e-mail: search@uar.co.uk

Debt advice

National Debtline

Tel: 0808 808 4000
website: www.nationaldebtline.co.uk

Consumer Credit Counselling Service

Tel: 0800 138 111
website: www.cccs.co.uk

Citizens Advice Bureau
Look in *Yellow Pages* for local office
website: www.citizensadvice.org.uk

Student Loans Company
100 Bothwell Street
Glasgow G2 7JD

Tel: 0800 40 50 10
website: www.slc.co.uk

Tax

Inland Revenue
Look under 'Inland Revenue' in local directories for nearest
    office
website: www.inlandrevenue.gov.uk

Tel: general enquiry line: 0207 667 4001
        self assessment helpline: 0845 9000 444
        children's tax credit helpline: 0845 300 3900

Home maintenance

Women & Manual Trades
52–54 Featherstone Street
London EC1Y 8RT

Tel: 0207 251 9192
website: www.wamt.org
e-mail: info@wamt.org

Index